PUB WAL

The Ickn
Path

TWENTY CIRCULAR WALKS IN
BUCKINGHAMSHIRE, BEDFORDSHIRE
HERTFORDSHIRE, ESSEX
CAMBRIDGESHIRE AND SUFFOLK

James A. Lyons

COUNTRYSIDE BOOKS
NEWBURY, BERKSHIRE

First published 1996

COUNTRYSIDE BOOKS
3 Catherine Road
Newbury, Berkshire

ISBN 1 85306 385 1

For the Icknield Way Association

Designed by Mon Mohan
Cover illustration by Colin Doggett
Photographs by the author
Maps by S. R. Lyons

Produced through MRM Associates Ltd., Reading
Typeset by Acorn Bookwork, Salisbury
Printed by J.W. Arrowsmith Ltd., Bristol

Contents

Publisher's Note

We hope that you obtain considerable enjoyment from this book; great care has been taken in its preparation. However, changes of landlord and actual closures are sadly not uncommon. Likewise, although at the time of publication all routes followed public rights of way or permitted paths, diversion orders can be made and permissions withdrawn.

We cannot of course be held responsible for such diversion orders and any inaccuracies in the text which result from these or any other changes to the routes nor any damage which might result from walkers trespassing on private property. We are anxious though that all details covering the walks and the pubs are kept up to date and would therefore welcome information from readers which would be relevant to future editions.

Introduction

The *Pub Walks along . . .* series describes circular pub walks that incorporate the best stretches of a long-distance path, plus links that serve as a useful guide to the overall route.

This particular book follows the Icknield Way Path, part of the Icknield Way, the oldest road in Britain. Today, a combination of waymarked, long-distance paths shadow the line of the ancient route which consisted of a broad band of loosely connected tracks running all the way from Dorset to the Wash. The Icknield Way Path starts where the Ridgeway National Trail ends, at Ivinghoe Beacon in Buckinghamshire, and runs for over 100 miles to Knettishall Heath, on the Suffolk/Norfolk border. Here, it links up with the Peddars Way National Trail, which continues to Hunstanton on the Wash and then along the Norfolk Coastal Path to Cromer.

The Icknield Way Association is the original body which devised and promoted a route for walkers along the Icknield Way. Following a successful campaign to gain official recognition for the route, the Icknield Way Path, as currently waymarked, was adopted in 1992 as a Regional Recreational Route by the Countryside Commission and the six counties crossed by the long-distance path. The route passes through Buckinghamshire, Bedfordshire, Hertfordshire, Essex, Cambridgeshire and Suffolk. In some places sections of the ancient route have inevitably disappeared under tarmac or have been obliterated by urban development. However, tracks along many of its most attractive parts still survive and in Bedfordshire, where the Historic Route (described in the Appendix) runs through Dunstable and Luton, the alternative Scenic Route is followed in this book. Also, at the Suffolk end of the Icknield Way Path various proposals on improving the route have been pending for some while and, in the meantime, the Icknield Way Association's Guide shows an alternative to the waymarked route through King's Forest. However, this book follows the existing, waymarked route throughout. There are no pubs along the last 17 miles and this 'Last Leg', therefore, is described as a separate, final, stage for those wanting to complete the long-distance route.

A flint axe logo is used to waymark the Icknield Way Path, which is well signed and generally in good condition, although some of the sunken tracks can be very muddy in winter. A waymarked riders' route coincides from time to time, but it is the walkers' route that is described in this book. Other rights of way incorporated into the circular pub walks follow the standard waymarking of arrows in the appropriate colour – yellow for footpaths, blue for bridleways, and red for byways.

The circular pub walks vary in length from 2½ miles to 6½ miles. All the longer routes have shorter options, whilst a combination of links and extensions can provide the basis for walks to suit individual requirements. The pubs vary from tiny village 'locals' to town pubs, from thatched pubs in a riverside setting to country inns. For the pub walks all that is needed is a pair of stout shoes or boots and a copy of this book! However, please remember that the sketch maps included are designed as simple guides for the starting points of the walks and an overall view of the routes. For those who wish to use detailed maps, the relevant Ordnance Survey Landranger sheet is recommended and listed in the preamble to each pub walk. More information on the long-distance path, including accommodation, can be obtained from the addresses shown at the end of the book.

Lastly, this book has been prepared jointly with my wife, Sally, who drew the sketch maps and shared in every stage of its preparation. Together, we walked the Way in search of the best combination of pubs and paths – may you enjoy the hostelries, the walks and the countryside along the Icknield Way Path as much as we did!

James A. Lyons
Spring 1996

Key for maps

●●●●●●●●●●●●●●●	Icknield Way Path
○○○○○○○○○○○○○○○	Icknield Way Path (Historic Route)
11	Location of Pub Walk
→ → →	Pub Walk
→●●●→●●●	Pub Walk incorporating Icknield Way Path

Icknield Way Path – Overall route from Ivinghoe Beacon to Knettishall Heath, Suffolk (112 miles)

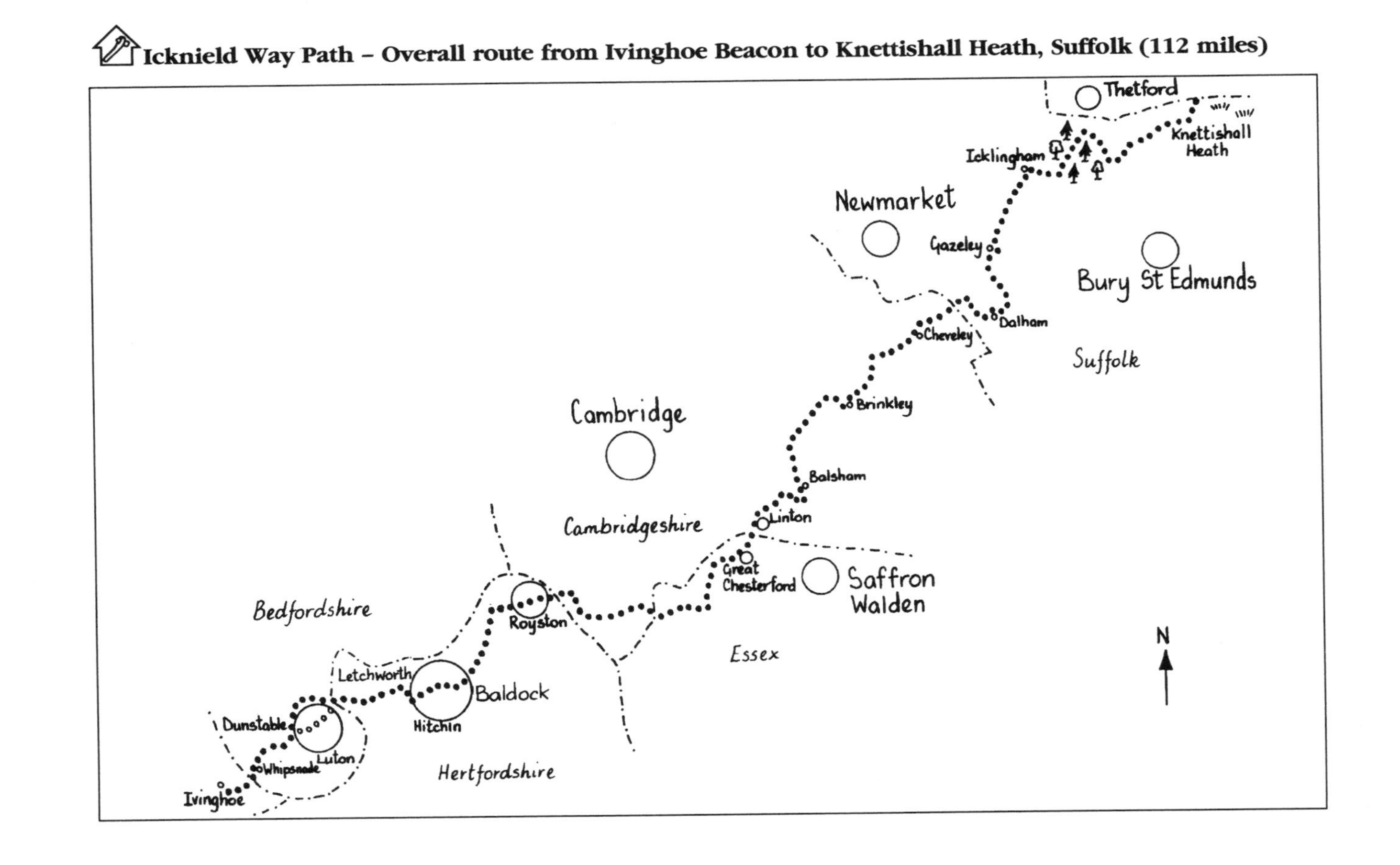

Icknield Way Path – Ivinghoe, Buckinghamshire to Ickleford, Hertfordshire (32 miles)

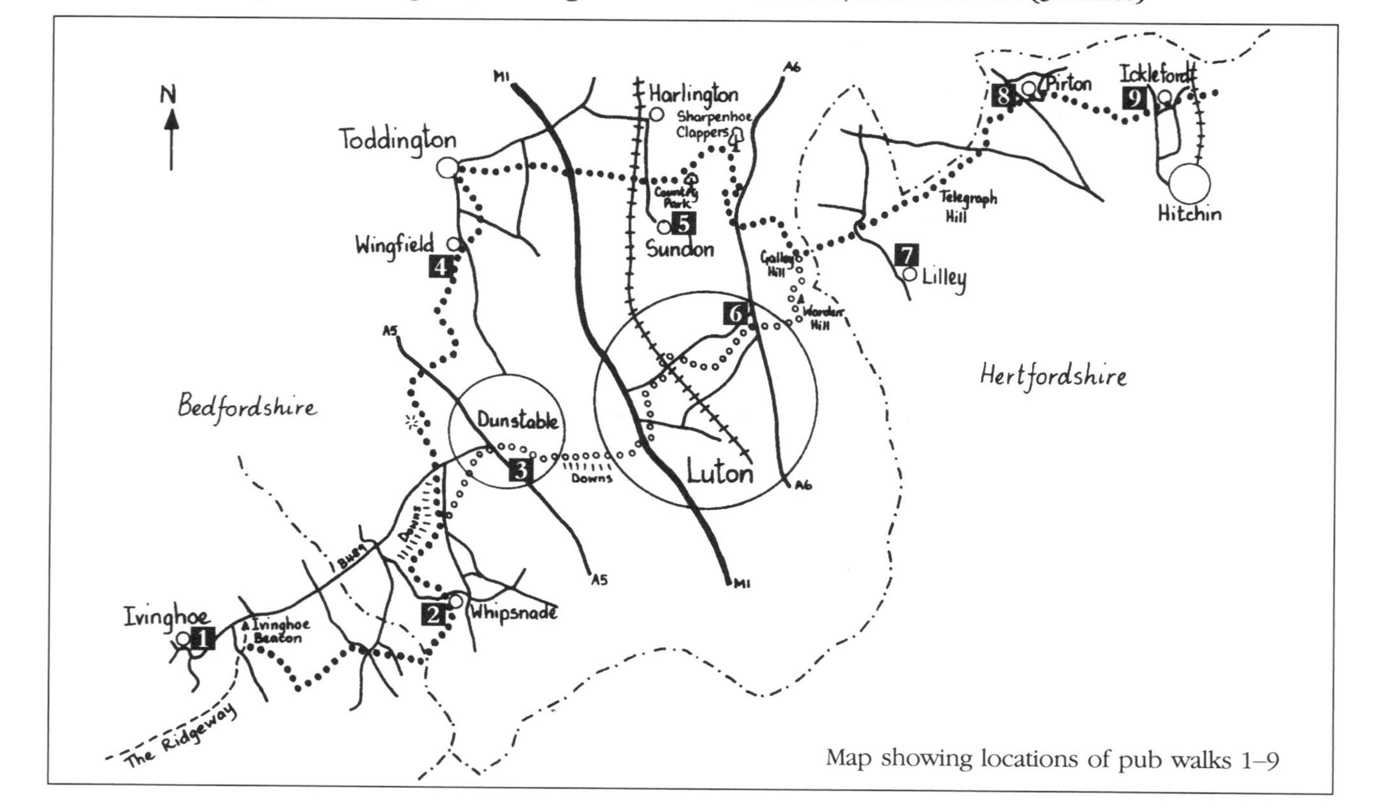

Map showing locations of pub walks 1–9

Icknield Way Path – Ickleford to Elmdon, Essex (26 miles)

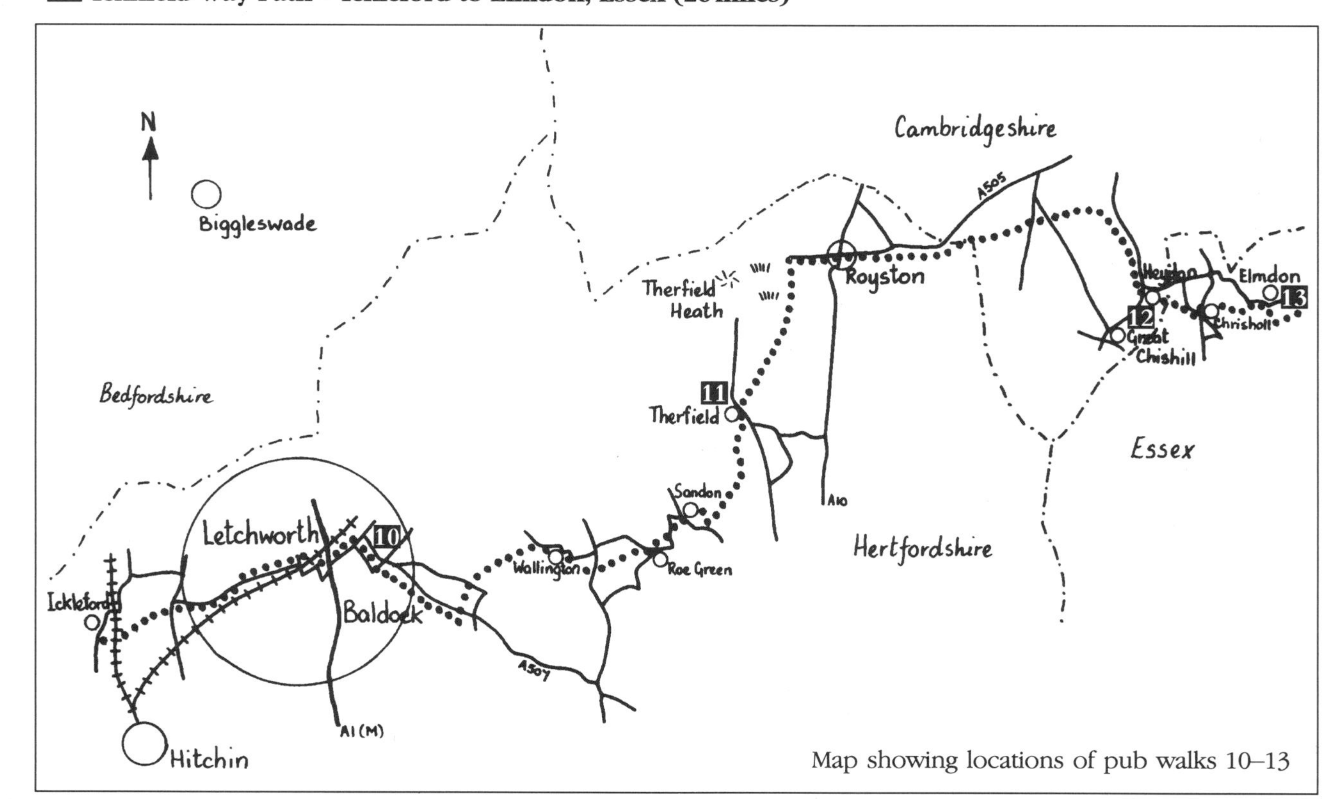

Map showing locations of pub walks 10–13

Icknield Way Path – Elmdon to Brinkley, Cambridgeshire (22 miles)

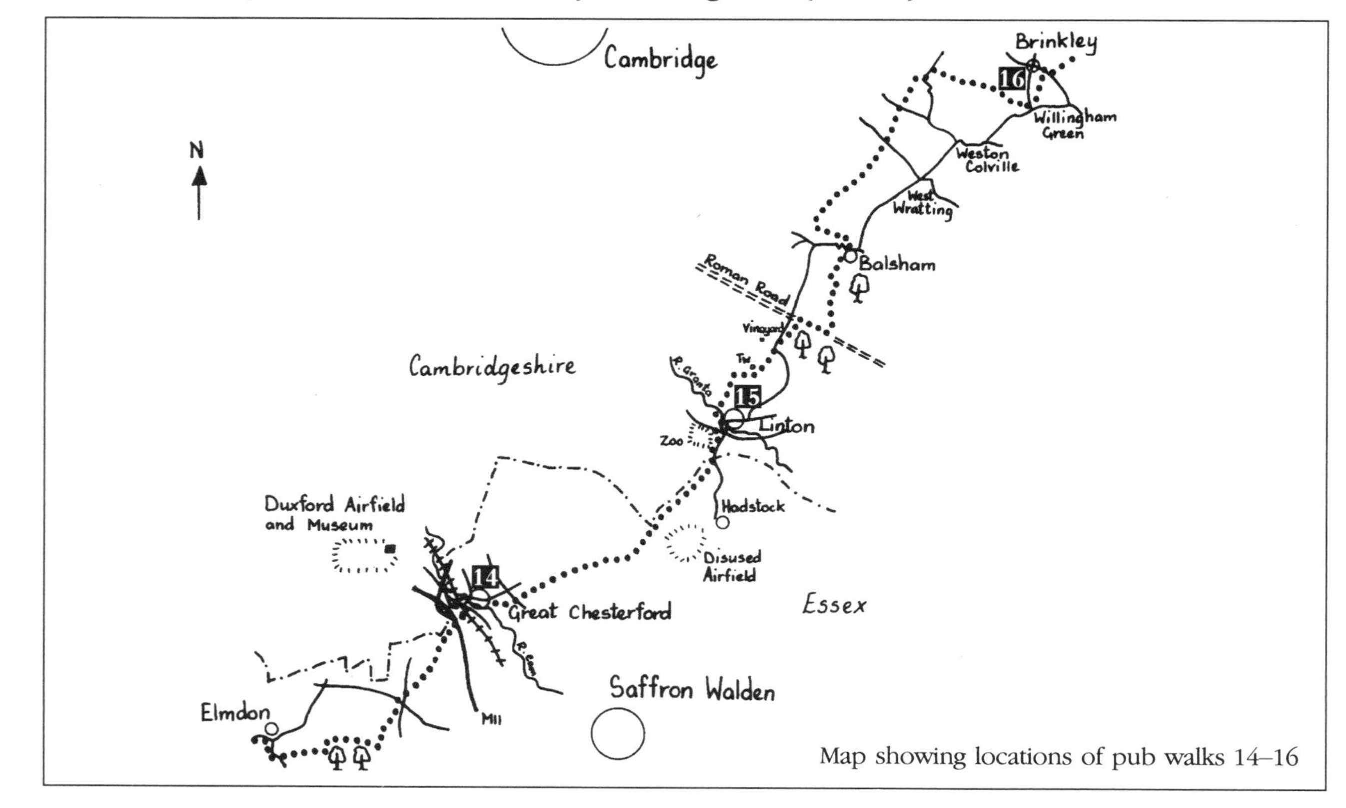

Map showing locations of pub walks 14–16

Icknield Way Path – Brinkley to Knettishall Heath, Suffolk (32 miles)

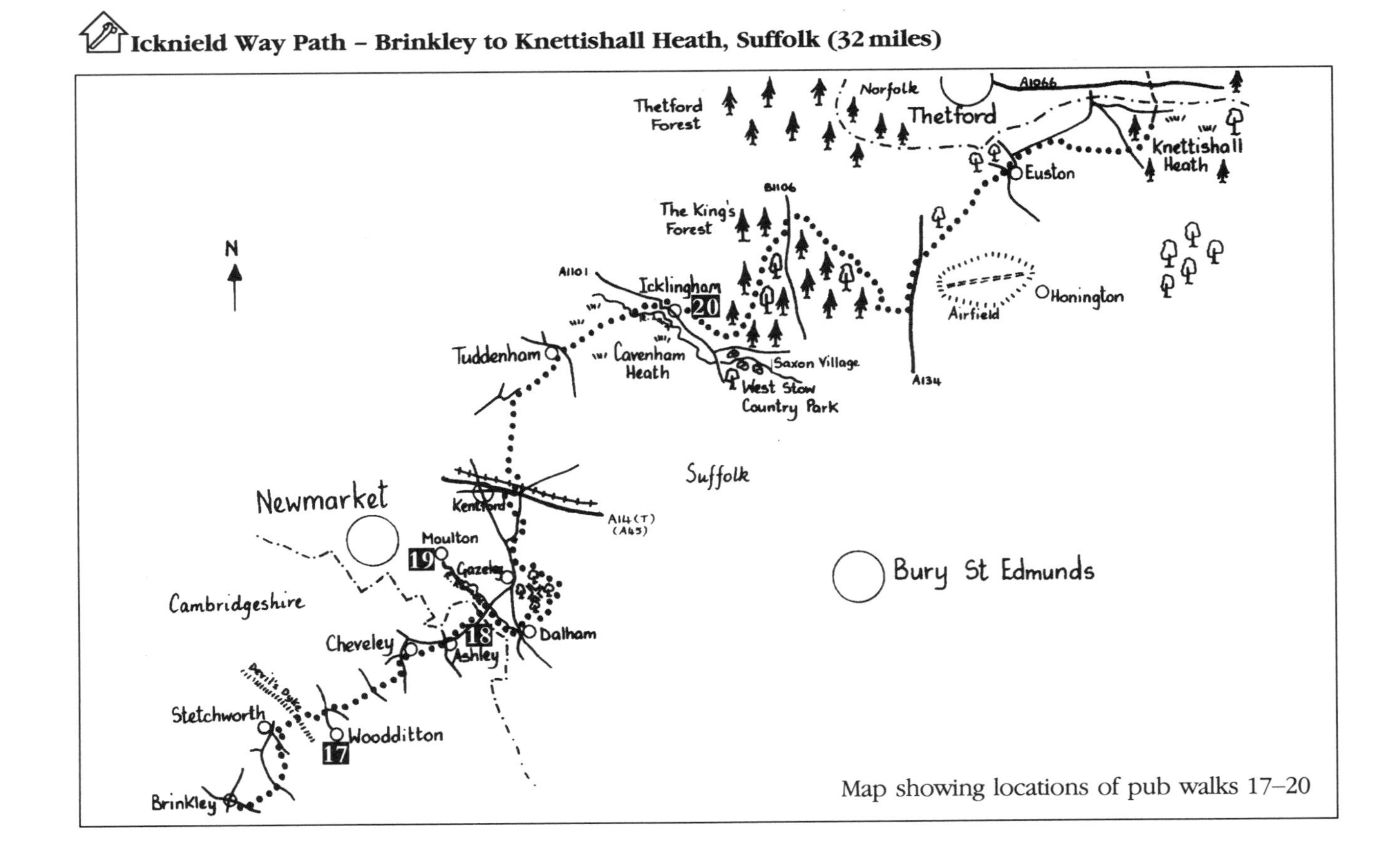

Map showing locations of pub walks 17–20

[1] **Ivinghoe** (Buckinghamshire)
The Rose and Crown

Ivinghoe lies below Ivinghoe Beacon, which marks the end of the Ridgeway National Trail and the start of the Icknield Way Path. It is an attractive village and has Buckinghamshire's only working watermill, with the oldest surviving post mill in England in nearby Pitstone. In addition to its other attractions, youth hostel accommodation makes Ivinghoe an ideal starting point for the Icknield Way Path.

The Rose and Crown, a small 'local' tucked away in the backstreets near the church, has its own claim to fame. Bernard Miles once lived in Ivinghoe and based his rustic monologues on 'happenings' in the village. For those who remember the monologues, regularly requested on *Children's Choice* in more innocent, radio days, this is *the* Rose and Crown – the pub made famous by the story of the wheelbarrow parked outside throughout an entire Sunday lunchtime, its load steaming gently in the sun ...

Today, inside the pub's modest, red-brick exterior, two separate bars serve customers in search of a good pint and home-cooking. Generous portions of pub grub include such dishes as cottage pie or chicken curry whilst for vegetarians there is a choice of pasta dishes or vegetable chilli. The pub does not have a garden, but there are some picnic-style tables in front and a small courtyard to the rear. The Rose and Crown is a freehouse and serves Adnams Bitter, Morrells Mild, Greene King IPA, Tetley Bitter and, appropriately enough for those setting out on the Icknield Way Path, Tring Brewery's Old Icknield. Murphy's Irish Stout, cider and two lagers are also available on draught.

The opening times are Monday to Saturday from noon to 2.30 pm and 6 pm to 11 pm, and on Sunday from noon to 10.30 pm. Meals are not served at lunchtime on Wednesdays.

Telephone: 01296 668472.

How to get there: Ivinghoe lies at the junction of the B489 and the B488, 5 miles south of Leighton Buzzard and 5 miles west of Dunstable. The pub is in Vicarage Lane, a small turning opposite the church.

Parking: There are roadside lay-bys in front of the pub.

Length of the walk: 4 miles. Map: OS Landranger 165 Aylesbury and Leighton Buzzard (inn GR 945164).

A walk (gentle option available) up to Ivinghoe Beacon, over 700 ft above sea level, with stupendous, panoramic views across open countryside and along the rolling line of the Chilterns. In addition, on Sundays during the summer, a visit to Ivinghoe could include the village's working watermill and the National Trust's restored windmill close by in Pitstone.

The Walk

From the pub the walk turns right, along the road leading to Ivinghoe Golf Club. Past the entrance to the golf club, it continues ahead on a hedged bridletrack which can be muddy in places at any time of the year. Eventually, the track reaches more open countryside with good views on both sides. The line of the Chiltern Hills dominates the landscape on the right, from the base of which arable farmland extends into the distance on the left, whilst ahead the square tower of Edlesborough church on its knoll serves as a prominent landmark. Crabtree Cottage, one-time home of Bernard Miles, is passed on the right, after which the track follows the drive from the cottage to the road above Ivinghoe Aston.

Here, the walk joins the Two Ridges Link (which joins the Ridgeway National Trail with the Greensand Ridge Walk across Bedfordshire) as it turns right, and follows the road uphill. Opposite the entrance to the old quarry workings, the walk turns right again, on a path heading for Ivinghoe Beacon across wide, arable fields. In the top corner of the second field it goes right, along a busy main road for about 50 yards, before turning left, along a minor road leading to Ivinghoe Beacon. Over a cattle-grid, the path turns left, straight up the face of Beacon Hill. The climb is steep, but not as bad as it looks, with plenty of resting places on

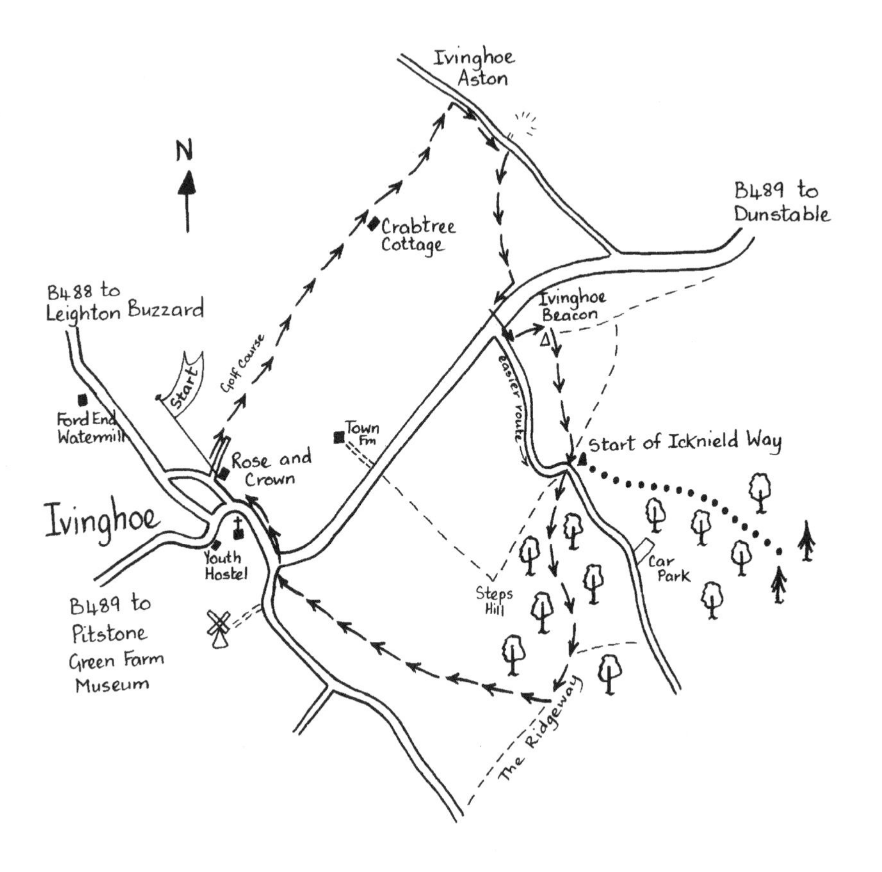

the way up! The road ahead presents a gentler challenge for those who prefer an easier route, (turn left at a right-hand bend towards the top of the hill, and follow the main track which leads back to the summit of the Beacon – see sketch-map).

Whichever route is chosen, the panoramic views from the top are a magnificent reward for the effort of getting there. At over 700 ft, the summit of the Beacon, ringed by the single bank and ditch of an Iron Age hill fort, marks the end of the Ridgeway National Trail. From the Ridgeway marker and nearby trig point, the walk bears right, along a track which roller-coasts along the top of the hill before dipping down to meet the road left earlier.

Just before the road, a path on the left runs from a National Trust information board to a stile and a milestone, where the Icknield Way Path begins its journey of over 100 miles to Knettishall Heath, near Thetford, on the Suffolk/Norfolk border.

The pub walk, however, passes by the start of the long-distance route and keeps ahead, across the road and over a stile, to follow a path below the summit of Steps Hill. From here, Marsworth Reservoir gleams in the distance, whilst, closer by, the cement works looms over the landscape, dwarfing Pitstone windmill. Over another stile the path turns left, along a fence, before emerging from scrub to follow round the edge of Incombe Hole. From here the walk crosses a sheep pasture to a stile in the hedge, across which the Ridgeway National Trail continues ahead. However, without going over the stile, the walk turns right, and follows the hedge down to and over another stile. From here the path clips the bottom corner of the field to a last stile, over which the walk follows a field-edge path to the left of a high hedge. From the corner of the field a fenced path leads to a road along which the route turns right.

Keeping ahead at a T-junction, the walk follows the road as far as Vicarage Lane, opposite the church, along which it turns right, back to the pub.

Icknield Way Path – Ivinghoe Beacon to Whipsnade (5½ miles)

A memorable start followed by pleasant walking across rolling, wooded countryside, ending with close encounters of a zoological kind.

From the official start (see flint axe logo in the pub walk description), the route first crosses upland, arable fields in a basin of hills. After running through mixed woodland and 'tunnelling' through a cypress plantation, it leaves the track and follows a fence ahead, up a steep hill. Clear of the woods at the top it turns left, in front of farm buildings, and runs down to the farm road from Hog Hall Farm, which it follows to the road, the A4146.

Here, the route turns right, through Dagnall. Past the Red Lion and over the crossroads, it continues to just past The Golden Rule, opposite which it turns left, through a small car park. From here a path is followed ahead to another road, along which the route turns right for about 50 yards then left, through a gate and along a path which runs uphill to a golf course. Here it follows waymarked posts down the centre of the golf course, before it turns left, and crosses into Bedfordshire as it keeps ahead to a hedge. After turning right, along the hedge for a short distance, it turns left, along a path following the perimeter fence of Whipsnade Wild Animal Park. Herds of deer and bison are in clear view on the other side of the fence with more exotic animals in the distance. Eventually, the path meets a narrow lane, along which the route turns left and continues past the Chequers Inn. From here the route is described in the next pub walk.

[2] **Whipsnade** (Bedfordshire)
The Chequers Inn

Whipsnade stands each side of a wide green and is best known for the nearby Whipsnade Wild Animal Park, which first opened as a zoo in 1931.

The Chequers, facing onto the village green, is a substantial 1930s-style brick building. It has a large, bright bar and cheerful furnishings complemented by pine tables and chairs. Shelves laden with a surprising variety of mainly pre-war bric-à-brac and domestic trivia provide an interesting topic of conversation, whilst what wall space is left displays a range of curios, from an ancient twelve-bore shotgun to an even more ancient cricket bat. Accommodation is spacious enough to allow for a separate dining room in which there are over 26 home-cooked meals on offer, ranging from traditional steak and kidney pie to Malaysian chicken on white rice. For something different again, the chicken in creamy cheese sauce, on a bed of chopped spinach, onions and cottage cheese, is highly recommended. Children are welcome and may, within reason, make up their own menu. Meals are not served on Sunday evenings during the winter months.

The pub has three resident dogs. Visiting canines are allowed in the bar, but not the restaurant. There is a large garden to the rear of the inn, complete with aviary and an adventure play area for children. As a special concession to walkers, the landlord is amenable to overnight camping within the garden area by back-packing customers.

The Chequers is a freehouse and serves Charles Wells Bombardier, Boddingtons Bitter, Whitbread Best Bitter and Webster's Yorkshire Bitter. During the summer an extra beer is on offer, usually Charles Wells Fargo. Guinness, cider and lager are also available on draught.

The opening times are Monday to Saturday from noon to 3 pm and 5 pm to 11 pm, and on Sunday from noon to 10.30 pm.

Telephone: 01582 873239.

How to get there: Whipsnade is on the B4540, off the A5 (Dunstable to St Albans). It also can be easily reached from Dunstable town centre via the B4541 (follow the signs for Whipsnade Wild Animal Park). The Chequers is on the southern side of the village green.

Parking: There is a large car park in front of the inn.

Length of the walk: 4½ miles (short-cut available). Map: OS Landranger 166 Luton, Hertford and surrounding area (inn GR 011178).

A memorable walk from the highest village in Bedfordshire to Dunstable Downs, with the highest views.

The Walk

From the inn the walk turns right, and follows the route of the Icknield Way Path along a path which keeps to the right of the village green. Over the road, it continues along a service road in front of cottages facing the green. Just past the last cottage it bears right, on a track waymarked for the Tree Cathedral and the Icknield Way. Through a small car park and swing-gates, the routes bears left, past the avenue of trees which mark the main entrance to the Tree Cathedral.

The area was established by E. K. Blyth in the 1930s in memory of friends killed in World War I. Over 25 different species of trees have been planted in the approximate floor-plan of a cathedral and, although it is not consecrated, there is an annual commemorative service here in the summer. The Tree Cathedral is now in the care of the National Trust and an information board next to the entrance gives full details.

Past the Tree Cathedral, the walk follows a grassy path to a stile in the corner. From here it goes alongside a fence behind Dell Farm Residential Centre. The centre organises rural studies for Bedfordshire schoolchildren and, on the other side of the fence, there is usually an interesting selection of rare breeds and semi-domesticated farm animals.

Over another stile in the corner the walk turns right, past a bungalow, along a wide track. The track becomes more of a sunken lane as it runs

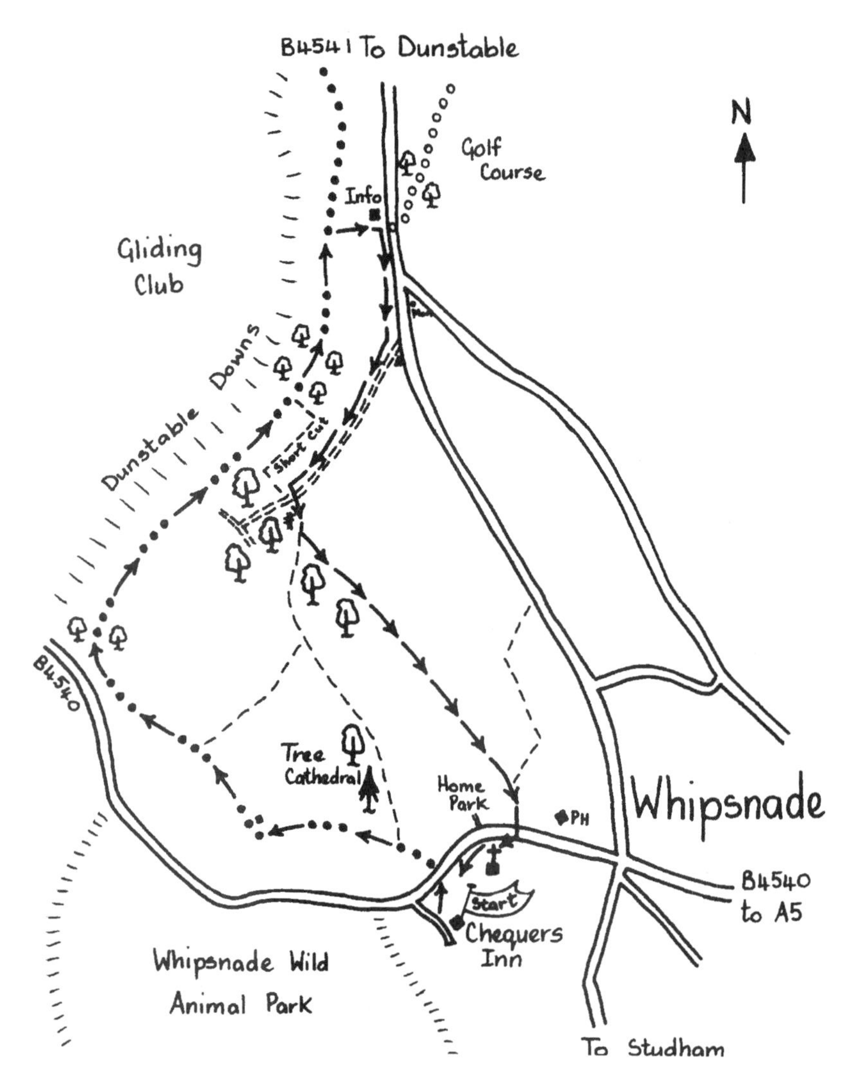

uphill, and this stretch can be muddy during winter months. At the top of the rise a gap opens up to reveal panoramic views across the plain below and along the line of the hills beyond Ivinghoe Beacon, the starting point of the Icknield Way Path.

Here, the walk bears right, then left, down through scrub and over a track. Within a few yards, it turns right, along a bridleway signposted to Dunstable Downs, and past a stile on the left where a National Trust notice board gives details of land management in this area of the downs. A swing-gate ahead gives access to the open downland and the walk continues ahead, just below the brow of the escarpment. After an exhilarating stretch of unenclosed hillside, the walk goes through another swing-gate, at which point a short-cut can be taken by turning right, up the hill (see sketch map).

The main walk, however, continues ahead and emerges from a belt of scrub on open hillside again. The path runs ahead to an Icknield Way Association information board, from which the walk angles right, up to the Information Centre. From here the headquarters of the London Gliding Club is in plain sight below, at the foot of the downs, and the view of gliders being winched or towed aloft is all the more enjoyable for a cup of tea from the refreshment kiosk!

From the Information Centre the walk leaves the Icknield Way Path as it turns right, keeping to the open grassland to the right of the road. At a fork in the road, on the other side, stands the second memorial seen on this walk to men who died in the First World War. Past the glider emergency landing ground, marked out with short, wooden posts, the walk continues ahead as far as a trig point where it turns right, along a surfaced farm access road. On the other side of open fields the walk turns off left, on a footpath running along the edge of a wood. In front of the wireless telegraph mast on the right, it bears left, on a path inside the edge of the woods. Clear of the trees, it follows a path to the left of a hedge before bearing to the right of a fence. A hedged, sunken track runs down the side of chalet-style homes, past which it keeps ahead at a junction to emerge on a strip of common land bordering a road.

Over the road, the walk turns right and passes the church of St Mary Magdalene, worth a visit for the charming simplicity of its interior. From here, the route continues ahead for the short distance back to the Chequers.

Icknield Way Path – Whipsnade to Dunstable Downs (2 miles)

A short stretch along the downs with some of the best views in Bedfordshire.

For the route from Whipsnade to Dunstable Downs, see above.

From the Information Centre the Icknield Way Path divides into two routes, the Historic Route and the Scenic Route. The Historic Route shadows the line of the original route but, in order to do so, has to traverse miles of urban sprawl through Dunstable and Luton. The Scenic Route detours around the conurbation and lives up to its name by crossing some of the finest walking country in Bedfordshire, and it is this route which is followed in this book. The Historic Route between Dunstable and Luton is briefly described in the Appendix. From the Information Centre, where the Scenic Route begins, the route is described in the next pub walk.

[3] **Dunstable** (Bedfordshire)
The White Swan Inn

Sited at the crossing of the Icknield Way and Watling Street, Dunstable has a long history as an important staging post for travellers.

The White Swan, affectionately known to its regulars as 'the mucky duck', dates back to before 1769, when it was sold and described as 'late The Two Black Boys'. At some time in its history part of the cellar was used as a town lock-up, complete with brick 'bunks' and small iron grills to the pavement above. Today, the establishment is run as an attractive town pub by a landlord who takes pride in its success at every level – as witnessed by the numerous sporting trophies on display. Sporting prints also decorate the walls, whilst an open fireplace puts the finishing touch to a comfortably furnished, open-plan interior.

Home-cooked meals served at lunchtimes include soups, the popular Dirty Duck Delight – a hearty, mixed grill – and lighter dishes such as Spanish omelette. A wide variety of sandwiches with generous fillings are regarded as a house speciality. Children are welcome and there is a choice of food for vegetarians. Meals are not available on Sundays, except for a barbecue during the summer months – weather permitting. There is a pleasant garden to the rear of the pub in spite of its proximity to the town centre. Dogs are not allowed indoors.

The White Swan is a freehouse and serves Marston's Pedigree Bitter, Boddingtons Bitter and Webster's Yorkshire Bitter. Courage Best Bitter, cider and five lagers are also available on draught.

Opening times are Monday to Saturday from 11 am to 11 pm, and on Sunday from noon to 10.30 pm.

Telephone: 01582 667833.

How to get there: Dunstable is on the main A5(T), just west of Luton. The pub is close to the centre of the town on the A5(T) (Watling Street).

Parking: Roadside parking is usually available on the slip road in front of the pub.

Length of the walk: 4 miles. Map: OS Landranger 166 Luton, Hertford and surrounding area (inn GR 023216).

A walk with spectacular views from Dunstable Downs, the highest viewpoint and the largest stretch of chalk downland in Bedfordshire.

The Walk

From the pub the walk crosses over the pelican crossing and turns right, along the High Street. Shortly, what was once an overhanging inn sign displays an extracted molar as an advertisement for its current line of business! The roadside path bears left and passes the Methodist church, then enters a small shopping precinct. Between here and the modern crossroads once stood no less than five inns and beer houses and, although these have long since disappeared, the town still boasts twelve pubs!

Past the church, the walk turns left, along the waymarked Icknield Way Historic Route. Behind the supermarket, it bears right, across the car park, then left, past a chapel and up to a T-junction to the right of the Salvation Army Community Centre. At this point it crosses the road and turns left along a fenced path which runs behind houses, then up the side of a recreation field to another road. Here, it keeps ahead, across the road, to follow a track running past allotments and a cemetery up to a road, along which the walk turns left. At a T-junction it turns right, and where the road bends left, it keeps ahead up a tarmac path. At a fork, it bears right and follows a path running uphill through scrub and, eventually, emerges on the edge of the fairway of Dunstable Downs Golf Club. From here the path continues ahead, aiming to the left of the clubhouse.

Along this stretch there are good views of Blows Down and north-east, across Dunstable and Luton, to the Warden Hills (see pub walk 6). After a small car park, the walk keeps ahead across the upper reaches of the golf course before running through more scrub to reach the road along the top of Dunstable Downs.

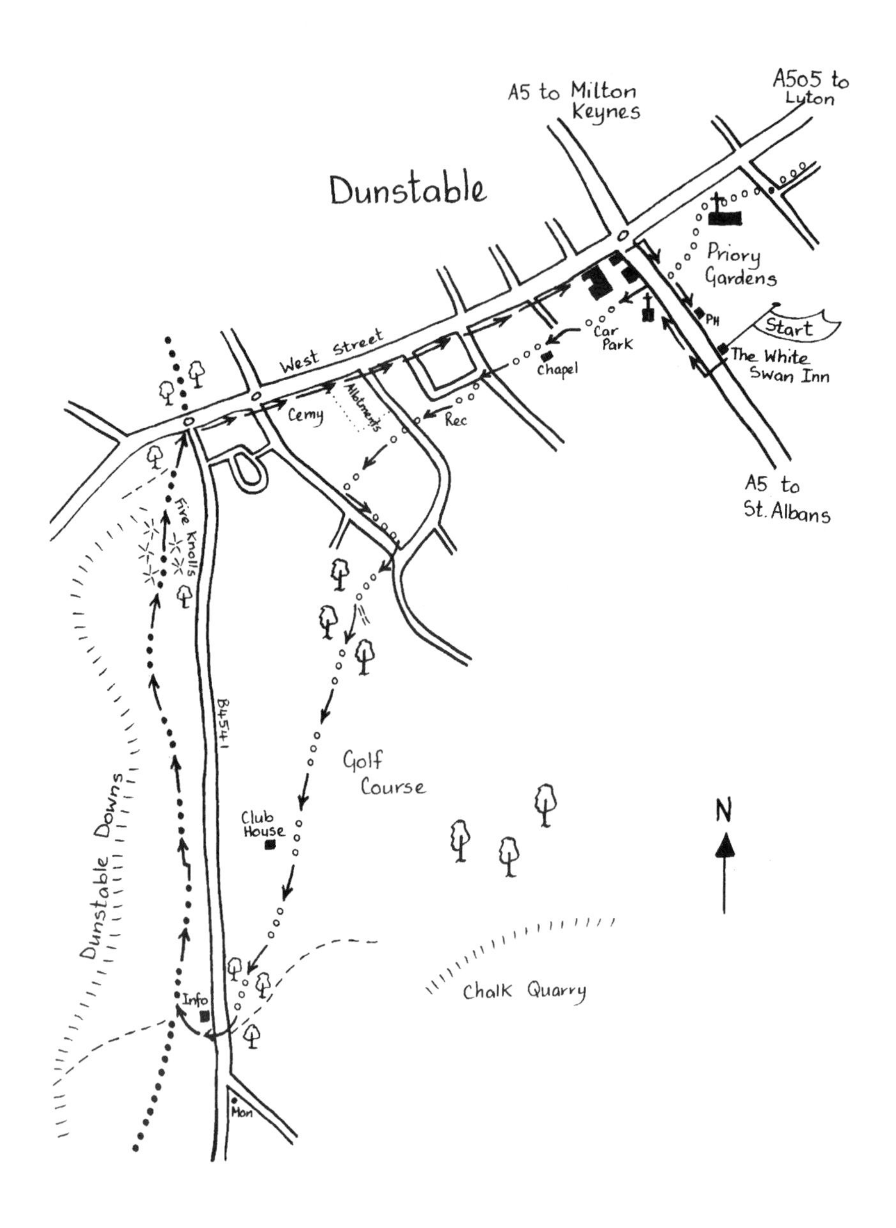

Here, the walk crosses the road diagonally to the right, through the car park to the Information Centre and shop, next to which a small kiosk serves refreshments. Ahead and below, the London Gliding Club provides a fascinating free show as gliders are winched and towed aloft. To the west, the view along the line of the hills extends beyond Ivinghoe Beacon, the start of the Icknield Way Path, whilst ahead, the downs continue for almost a mile as far as the Bronze Age burial mounds known as the Five Knolls.

From the Information Centre the walk turns right and follows the Icknield Way Path Scenic Route along the line of the downs. Through a swing-gate, it continues along a stretch regularly used for launching hang-gliders, beyond which the path leads past the Five Knolls tumuli, the northernmost of which was used in medieval times as the site for a gallows. Through another swing-gate, a grassy slope leads down to a roundabout where the Icknield Way Path crosses over the road, but the pub walk turns right, down West Street.

Past the main entrance to the cemetery and two more pubs, the walk arrives at the crossroads in the centre of Dunstable where it turns right for a few yards then left, over a pelican crossing. Having crossed the road, it turns right, past the entrance to Priory Gardens and the Church of St Peter, all that survives of the Augustinian Priory founded around 1131 by Henry I. The church's impressive west front dates from Norman and 13th-century times. The Icknield Way (Historic Route) continues from the rear of the church, but the pub walk keeps on along the High Street, past the Saracen's Head, once three inns and Dunstable's oldest surviving pub. Other buildings of historic interest passed along this short stretch of the High Street include a row of 18th-century almshouses, and Chew's House, originally a school for 40 Church of England boys, beyond which the walk arrives back at the pub.

Icknield Way Path (Scenic Route) – Dunstable Downs to Wingfield (6 miles)

This stretch begins with spectacular views and is followed by good walking across rolling, arable farmland.

For the route from the Information Centre on Dunstable Downs to West Street, see above. After crossing West Street just above the roundabout, the route continues along a track lined by mature beech trees on the right. Keeping ahead after the trees end, it turns right, at a cross-tracks with Maiden Bower, the site of an Iron Age hill fort, across the field to the left. Eventually, the track bears left and runs downhill before turning right, between the abutments of a dismantled railway bridge. From here it follows a narrow lane through Sewell (ignore the Icknield Way fingerpost indicating left, which takes the route along a short stretch of overgrown paths, difficult to walk and follow). Eventually, the lane meets the main A5(T), across which the route turns left for 50 yards or so, before bearing right, down a slip road opposite the Maiden Bower public house. The waymarked route is rejoined where it comes down steps on the left, after which the walk turns right, on a path up the side of Well Cottage. Clear of the houses and past the sewage works, it keeps ahead along the left-hand

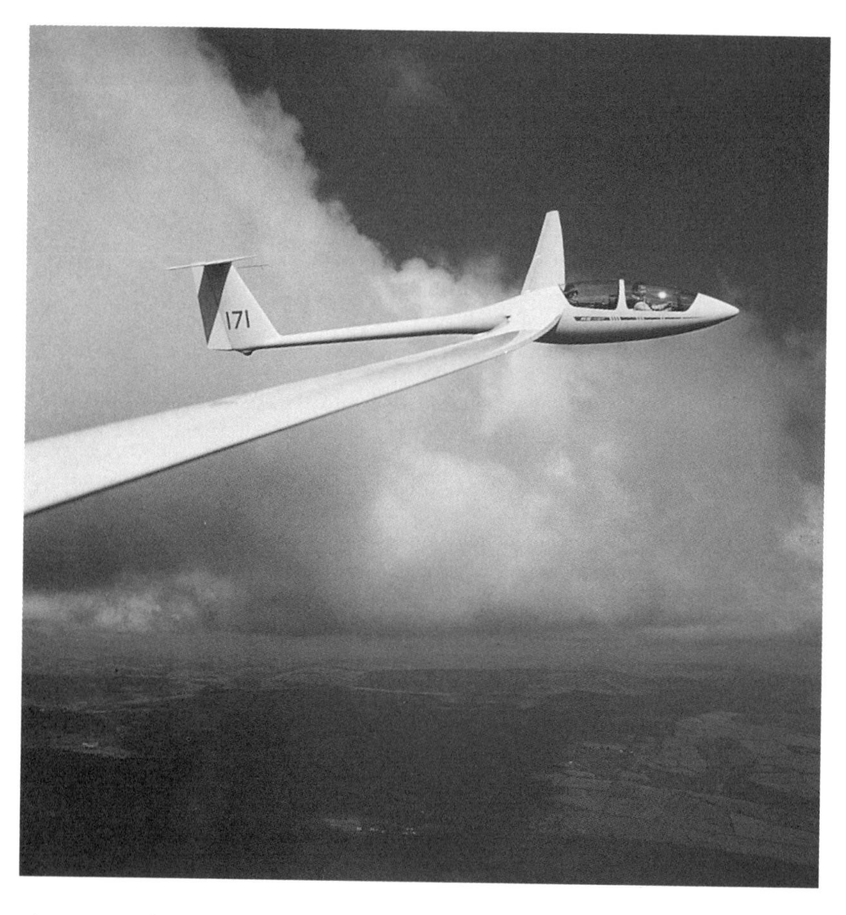

An unusual view of a glider over the London Gliding Club at Dunstable. (Photo: Tony Hutchings courtesy the London Gliding Club.)

side of a sloping, arable field to the far corner, from where a path continues along the edge of a wood. At a meeting of the ways, it turns left, along a concrete track, then left again, over a stile, to follow a path across arable fields to a road.

Over the road and a metal stile, the route keeps ahead along field-edge paths and past a national grid pylon before turning left, then right, up the side of another arable field. At the top of the rise it keeps to the right of a hedge, then follows a boundary fence and hedge round a cricket pitch to a road running through Wingfield. Here, the route turns right, and follows the road past the Plough Inn. From here the route is described in the next pub walk.

[4] **Wingfield** (Bedfordshire)
The Plough Inn

Wingfield is a small hamlet which, like so many Bedfordshire villages, enjoys a splendid feeling of rural isolation in spite of its proximity to more built up areas.

The thatched Plough, named after the constellation, was built in 1822 as a coaching inn to serve the carriage trade on the nearby main road. Inside, one bar serves an open-plan, L-shaped area with a separate games room to the rear. Homely, wooden tables and chairs are supplemented by built-in, comfortable settles with a wintertime open fire at one end of the bar and a log burner at the other. Behind the bar it's a question of 'every photograph tells a story' – ask the landlord, if he's not too busy and you're in no hurry to start the walk! Bar food includes double-decker sandwiches, baguettes or pitta bread, with a choice of generous fillings. Good-value-for-money, home-cooked meals range from quiche to chilli and 'specials' such as bacon steak, egg and chips, vegetarian dishes and, of course, traditional Sunday lunch. Meals are not served on a Sunday evening. To the rear of the pub is a very pleasant garden and children's play area.

The Plough is a freehouse with a good choice of real ales, including three local beers, Shefford Bitter, Shefford Wheat Beer and Shefford Black Bat. Other cask ales include Fuller's London Pride, Hop Back Mild, Smiles Best

Bitter and Eldridge Pope Royal Oak. Guinness, Bass Toby, lager and cider are also available on draught.

The opening times are Monday to Saturday from 11 am to 3 pm and 6 pm to 11 pm, and on Sunday from noon to 10.30 pm.

Telephone: 01525 873077.

How to get there: Wingfield is close to Tebworth, just 2 miles south-west of Toddington (near junction 12 of the M1). The pub is on the eastern edge of the hamlet and can be reached by minor roads from either the A5(T) (near Hockcliffe) or the A5120 (Toddington to Dunstable).

Parking: There is a car park opposite the pub.

Length of the walk: 6 miles (short-cut available). Map: OS Landranger 166 Luton, Hertford and surrounding area (inn GR 002263).

A walk across the fields to Toddington, which has eight pubs, the remains of a Norman motte and bailey, and Toddington Manor, a rare breeds centre. En route is the restored church at Chalgrave, which has medieval wall paintings and table tombs.

The Walk

From the pub the walk turns left and follows the route of the Icknield Way Path along the road. After a short distance, it turns left again, over a roadside stile. From here it crosses a pasture behind a house to another stile, where it bears left, across two wide, arable fields, aiming for a distant pylon. At the road it turns left, up to a crossroads, where it turns right, along a narrow lane leading to Chalgrave church.

All Saints' church is all that remains of one of the earliest settlements in Bedfordshire. The building suffered a long period of neglect following its abandonment but has undergone extensive restoration. There are also new seats in its lovingly tended churchyard from which to enjoy views of the church in its peaceful setting and across open countryside to the south.

From the rear of the churchyard, the walk turns right, and runs down the left-hand side of a new golf course. During wet weather a spring creates heavy going along the top end of this stretch, which continues down to a meeting of the ways at the bottom of the hill. Here, the short-cut turns right (see sketch map).

The main walk, however, turns left, over a footbridge and stile. From here several stiles and pastures are crossed to a road which the walk dog-legs across, right, then left. From the roadside stile the path angles left, over a first, small, pasture to another stile set in the hedge. From here the walk keeps ahead over several stiles and across more pastures, aiming to the right of the distant tower of Toddington church. Eventually, in the top

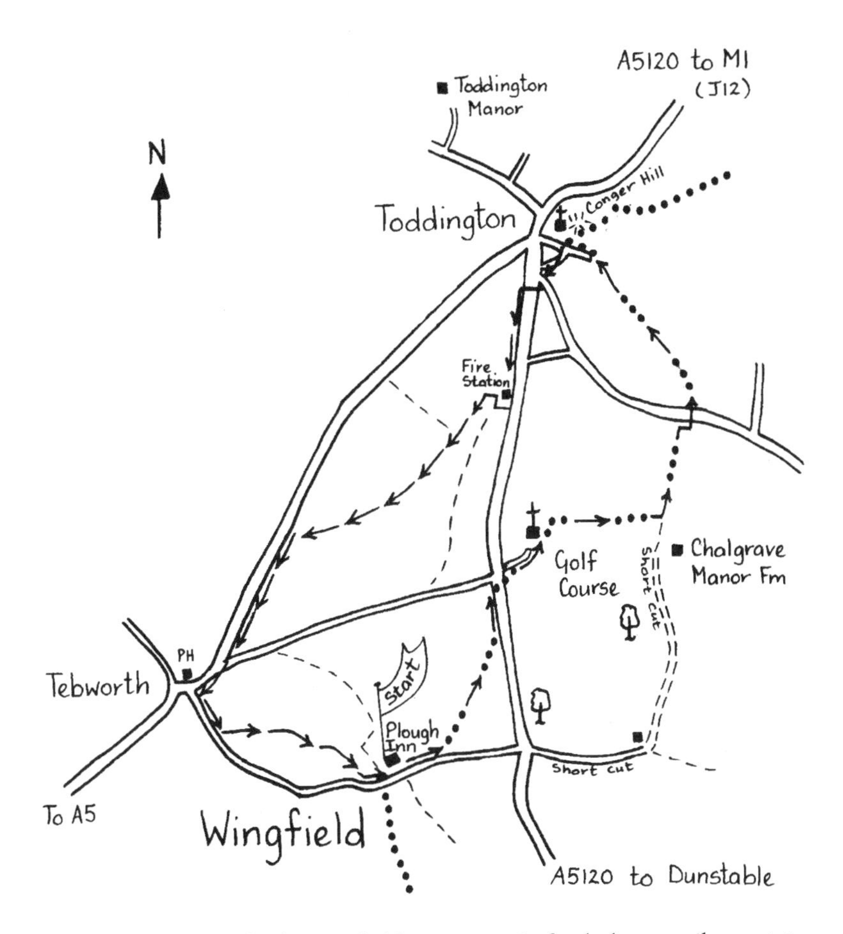

right-hand corner of a longer field, a stream is forded to a stile next to a metal gate, from where a hedged track runs uphill. Towards the top of the hill the track becomes Conger Lane, which is followed through houses on the outskirts of Toddington. Just before the Oddfellows Arms public house, the Icknield Way Path turns right, through a swing-gate, but the pub walk continues ahead to one of the best examples of a village green in Bedfordshire.

A large, cast-iron water pump stands on the green, which is faced by a row of thatched cottages next to St George's church, with a mixture of pubs, shops and houses on the other three sides. Here, the walk turns left, on a slip road along the edge of the green, past the front of the Oddfellows Arms and the library, beyond which it follows the High Street. Past a small garden and pond next to the Angel Inn, it crosses over the road to the Bedford Arms and continues down the High Street. Just past the small fire station it turns right, on a bridleway. After keeping to the left of a house, the path turns right, then left, in the corner behind the fire station. Bearing left in the next corner, it crosses over a footbridge and continues ahead to another footbridge and stile, over which it follows the left-hand side of a brook. Over a concrete bridge the field-edge path follows the water across several pastures before leaving it and crossing a last field to a road.

Here, the walk turns left, along the road, which is followed up a long rise then right, into Tebworth. Shortly before the Queen's Head is reached the walk turns left, along the Wingfield road. Just past the last house, it turns left, on a footpath across an arable field. Over a first stile, it follows a path in roughly the same direction across several paddocks before passing between houses to emerge on the road, in Wingfield. Here, the walk turns left, and follows the road back to the pub.

Icknield Way Path (Scenic Route) – Wingfield to before Sundon Hills Country Park (4 miles)

Easy walking over undulating, arable farmland each side of the M1, followed by rising ground flanking Sundon Hills Country Park.

For the route from Wingfield to Toddington, see above. At the top of Conger Lane, the route turns right, through a swing-gate, and keeps to the right of the motte and bailey mound to a gate in the corner. Here, it turns right, then left, on a fenced track running along the bottom of a cemetery. At the corner, it turns right, then follows the fence left, and continues downhill on a fenced path to cross stiles each side of a road.

From here the route keeps ahead and, over a footbridge, turns left on a track leading to a road. Here, it turns right and crosses over the M1 on the road to Old Park Farm. Just before the farm it turns right, over a stile, and crosses a yard. Past barns on the left, it bears right, along a track. At a waymarked post it turns left, across arable fields and past two National Grid pylons. From the second pylon a track turns right, then left, under the main railway line, before bearing right, along a hedged track. Eventually, the route turns right, along a field-edge, then left, in the corner. After following the sloping field up rising ground it turns right, at a waymarked post, along a path which keeps just inside the edge of the woods. The path runs uphill for a good distance to a gate on the edge of the woods, through which the route turns left. From here the route is described in the next pub walk.

[5] **Upper Sundon** (Bedfordshire)

The Red Lion

Upper Sundon is close to the Icknield Way Scenic Route and the Sundon Hills Country Park, which has 93 acres of north-facing chalk downs.

The Red Lion, built about 150 years ago, is one of three pubs in the village. Over the years extensions have provided spacious accommodation which allows for two separate bars, and a tiny 'snug' adjoining a games room. Photographs and prints in the 'snug' reflect the sporting interests of the regulars using the public bar and games room. The comfortably furnished lounge is decorated with photographs of old Dunstable and Luton, where the landlord once ran a pub. The Red Lion is widely known for the quality of its value-for-money home-cooking and welcomes children. Bar meals include ploughman's, brunch or quarter-pound burgers. The menu offers such favourites as steak and kidney pie, home-cooked ham or gammon steaks, daily 'specials', such as egg, bacon and cheese flan, plus a vegetarian selection and a choice of home-made desserts. Meals are not available on a Sunday night. There is a children's play area and garden to the rear of the pub, with a separate area for dogs.

The Red Lion is a freehouse and has a good selection of real ales, including Flowers IPA, Whitbread Best Bitter, Morland Old Speckled Hen, Boddingtons Bitter and Fuller's London Pride. Guinness, Whitbread Bitter and

Poacher, Bentley's Yorkshire Bitter, lager, and cider are also available on draught.

The opening times are Monday to Saturday from 11 am to 3 pm and 5 pm to 11 pm, and on Sunday from noon to 10.30 pm.

Telephone: 01525 875806.

How to get there: Upper Sundon is only 1 mile north of the outskirts of Luton, just east of the M1. The village is reached on minor roads off either the A6 (Bedford to Luton) or the A5120 (Ampthill to Dunstable). The pub is at the centre of the village.

Parking: There is a car park to the rear of the pub.

Length of the walk: 3½ miles (extension available). Map: OS Landranger 166 Luton, Hertford and surrounding area (inn GR 046278).

A walk through Sundon Hills Country Park in this Area of Outstanding Natural Beauty (AONB). The walk can be extended to Sharpenhoe Clappers, a National Trust nature reserve, from which there are panoramic views across open countryside.

The Walk

The walk starts by following a bridleway track down the right-hand side of the pub. Through a gate, it keeps ahead down to a swing-gate on the right, almost opposite a small sewage works. Through this gate, the path bears right, across a small, hillside pasture to pick up the Icknield Way Scenic Route at another swing-gate on the edge of a wood.

Here, the walk turns right, to the corner of the field, where it goes through the hedge and turns right again, along the hedge. At the corner of this large field, it turns left and follows the hedge for a good distance with wide views across open country to the north. From a swing-gate in the far corner of the field a short track leads to a road, along which the walk turns right. After 100 yards or so it turns left, through the entrance to Sundon Hills Country Park.

Here, the walk joins the start of the John Bunyan Trail, a newly-established, 45 mile long 'Pilgrim's Progress' through Bedfordshire. Beyond the car park and picnic site, the walk keeps to left of the hedge along the line of the hills. Ahead to the left, the beech trees on the spur of Sharpenhoe Clappers make a distinctive landmark, whilst there are occasional bench seats from which to enjoy the views from Bunyan's 'delectable mountains'.

Through a swing-gate the path skirts round behind a small combe and then runs up to a fence and gate. Without going through the gate, the walk turns right, over a stile and along a field-edge path to the far corner of a large, arable field. Here, the walk can be extended by turning left,

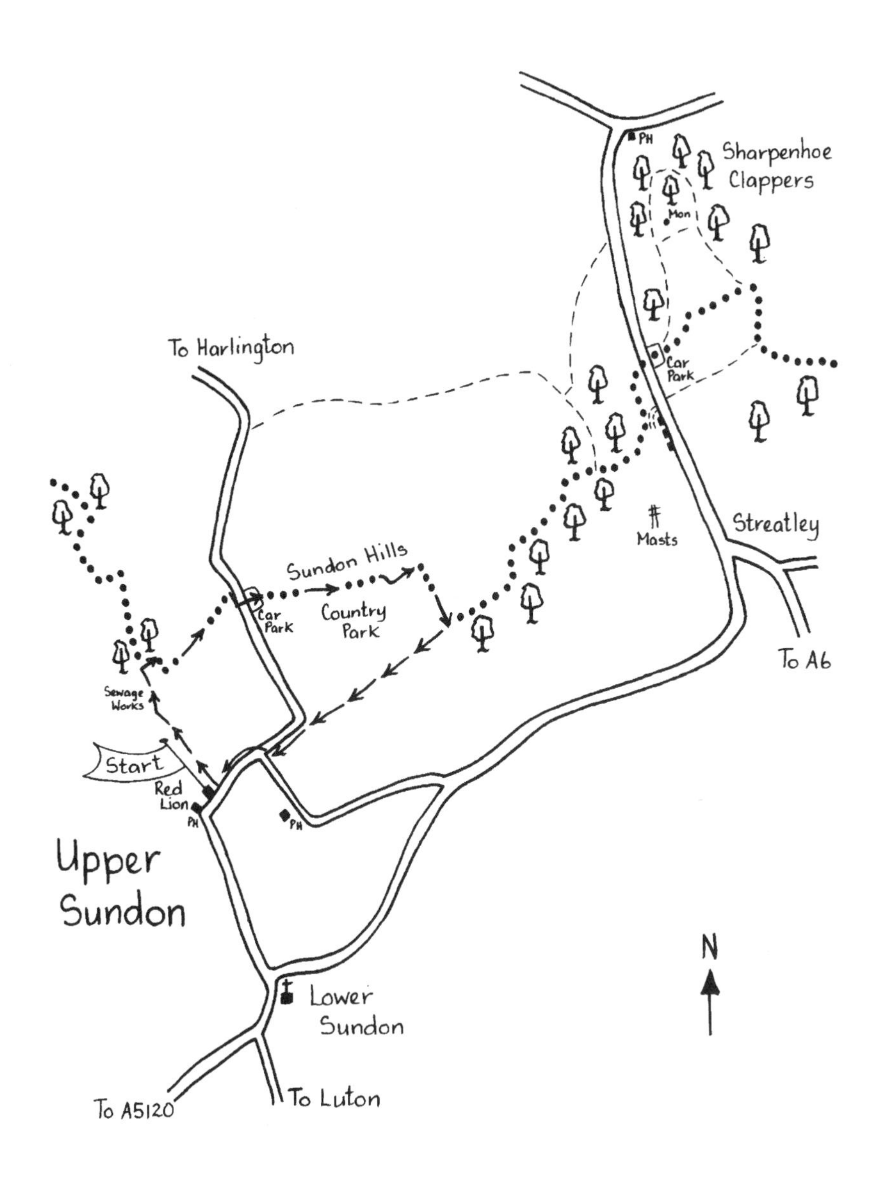

with the Icknield Way Path and the John Bunyan Trail (see sketch map), to Sharpenhoe Clappers.

The main walk, however, turns right, along a field-edge track which, eventually, leads to a road. Here, the walk bears left, and follows the road through the village, back to the pub.

Icknield Way Path (Scenic Route) – before Sundon Hills Country Park to Galley Hill (5 miles)

For the route through Sundon Hills Country Park, see above. From the T-junction where the pub walk turns right, the route turns left, along the edge of a wood, at the end of which it turns left again, along another track for a short distance. It then turns right, along the edge of another wood, then left, before bearing right, along a good path through the woods. At a junction it bears right, then left, along the edge of the trees, with an open field to the right. In the corner it goes through/over double metal fieldgates and bears right, across the top end of a pasture to a roadside stile.

Across the road, the route runs through a small car park on the boundary of Sharpenhoe Clappers. Past the National Trust information board, it first follows a tarmac path which becomes a track along the edge of a wood. At a waymarked post it turns right, over the rise of an open field and down to a stile. From here a path runs ahead through scrub before turning right and reaching an open area of hillside with wide views across the valley to the left. Eventually, the walk follows the path right, up to another stile over which it turns left, to the corner of the field. Here, it turns left again, down a wide track. A swing-gate on the left leads to a second gate through which the path turns right, sloping down the steep hillside. Steps almost at the bottom take it left, down to another gate, through which it crosses a wide pasture, heading for the bottom of the embankment of the A6. Over a footbridge it angles right, up the steep bank, and turns right, along the roadside path.

At a crossroads the route turns right, along the road into Streatley, then left, at a T-junction, to follow a one-way lane back to the main road. Over the road, it follows a track and power lines past Swedish Cottages. At the fifth pylon it turns right, to a wood where it rejoins the Historic Route of the Icknield Way at Galley Hill. From here the route is described at the end of the next pub walk.

[6] **Luton** (Bedfordshire)
The Warden

The Warden, named after the nearby hill, is situated on the northern fringes of Luton, Bedfordshire's biggest town. A large, 1930s, brick building, it had its own dance floor in pre-war days when well-known dance bands drew crowds from the town for the Saturday night 'hop'.

Today, the pub belongs to the Beefeater chain and the A6 provides the customers. Spacious, open-plan accommodation is comfortably furnished and served by a long bar. The old dance floor area has been converted into a restaurant serving good-value-for-money meals, which vary according to the season but always include such staples as hearty steaks or a variety of fish and chicken dishes. Among the bar meals are baguettes or jacket potatoes with various fillings, plus pastas or curries. There is a children's menu and a good selection of vegetarian meals. The restaurant is open throughout the week and is often supplemented by a weekend barbecue during the summer. There is a large garden which is well stocked with children's slides and other play equipment. Dogs are welcome in the garden, but not inside.

Cask ales on offer include Boddingtons Bitter and Flowers Original, plus a guest beer, such as Castle Eden Ale. Guinness, Murphy's, lager and cider are also available on draught.

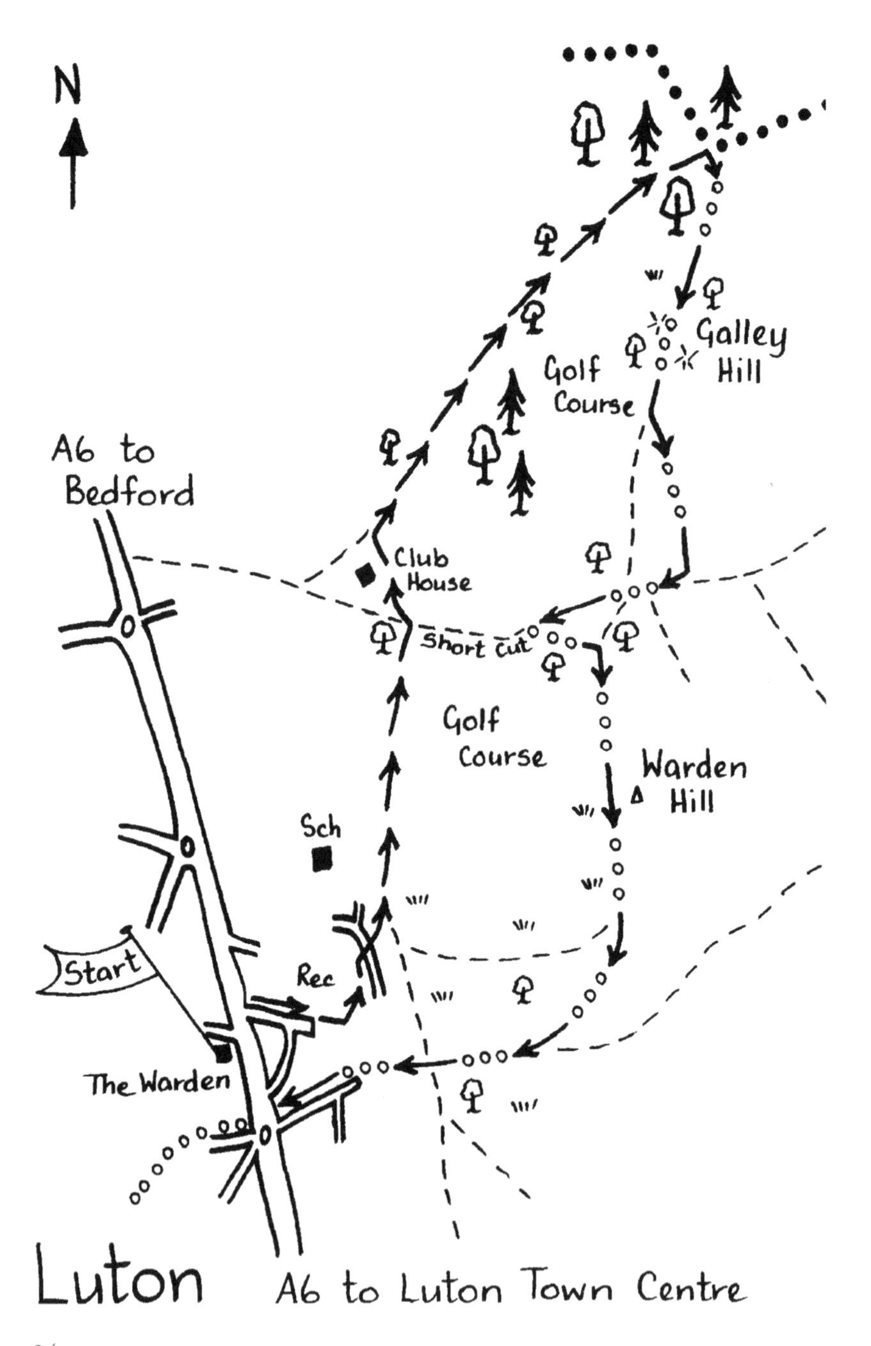
N
A6 to
Bedford
Club
House
Short Cut
Golf
Course
Galley
Hill
Golf
Course
Warden
Hill
Sch
Rec
Start
The Warden
Luton
A6 to Luton Town Centre

Opening times are Monday to Saturday from 11 am to 11 pm, and on Sunday from noon to 10.30 pm.
Telephone: 01582 591277.

How to get there: Luton, in southern Bedfordshire, can be reached from junctions 10 or 11 of the M1. The pub is on the A6 Luton to Bedford road, on the northern edge of the town.

Parking: There is ample parking to the front, side and rear of the pub.

Length of the walk: 4 miles (short-cut available). Map: OS Landranger 166 Luton, Hertford and surrounding area (inn GR 083255).

A memorable walk on which it is well worth taking binoculars for the panoramic views from the Galley and Warden hills.

The Walk

From the pub the walk crosses over the A6, and turns left, along the roadside path. After 50 yards or so, it turns right, down Hillcrest Avenue, at the end of which it keeps ahead, through a gap in the hedge, and turns left, along a fenced path. Across the end of a recreation field, the path leads to a road in front of houses facing Warden Hill. The walk keeps left as it crosses over the road, which is followed to just before a roadside car park and the main entrance to a school. Here, it turns right for a few yards then left, along a track to the right of a high hedge, with South Beds Golf Course stretching across to the foot of the hills on the right. The walk continues to follow the hedge on the edge of the golf course and, eventually, crosses over a main track. Here, a short-cut can be taken by turning right (see sketch map), across the golf course and the remains of Iron Age tribal boundaries known as Dray's Ditches.

The main walk, however, crosses over the track and bears left, behind a green, then keeps ahead as it joins a wide track running past the front of the clubhouse. At a T-junction it turns right, and follows a stony track between high hedges for about ½ mile. Eventually, the golf course ends on the left and the track climbs to a cross-tracks where the Icknield Way Scenic Route comes in from the left to rejoin the Icknield Way Historic Route, which comes in from the right.

At this meeting of the ways an Icknield Way Association information board provides details relating to the path and its historical background. From here the Icknield Way Path runs north-east, on the track ahead.

The pub walk, however, turns right, and follows the Historic Route back to Luton. After a few yards the walk bears right, across the upper end of the golf course, to a swing-gate which gives access to an area which, together with nearby Warden Hill, has been designated a Site of Special Scientific Interest (SSSI). Management includes the clearance of scrub, and dogs should be kept under close control within the fenced areas, where livestock have been reintroduced. From the gate the walk follows a path up to the top of Galley Hill, where the bumpy ground marks the remains of tumuli and the site of the gallows from which the hill gets its name. Excavations in this area have revealed some gruesome finds and indications of black magic rituals in the past.

From the top of the hill the path runs down to a swing-gate through which the walk continues along a field-edge path with fine views across Luton and open countryside. In the corner of the field it turns left (do not go through the gate) and continues to follow the edge of the field until meeting a track. Here, the walk turns right, and stays with the track as it runs downhill, ignoring turnings off to the left and right. Towards the bottom of the hill it crosses over a narrow neck of the golf course and continues along the track for a short distance before turning off sharply to the left, from where the short-cut rejoins the main walk.

Through a swing-gate, the walk follows a path almost to the top of Warden Hill, where it turns right, at a waymarked wooden post, on a path leading to another swing-gate. Through this, it follows a wire fence with wide views to the right, including ground below covered in the earlier stages of the walk. A trig point (around 600 ft above sea level) on the other side of the fence provides an excellent vantage point from which to enjoy wide views that stretch to the easily recognizable control tower at Luton airport on the horizon to the south-east. From the trig point the walk continues to follow the fence until it ends and from here it runs more or less ahead, down to take the second of two chalky paths on the right.

Through a last swing-gate at the bottom of the hill the walk follows a grassy track over rough pasture, on the other side of which it goes along Weybourne Drive to a roundabout on the A6. Here, the walk turns right, back to the pub.

Icknield Way Path – Galley Hill to Hertfordshire border (½ mile)

A short stretch following a green lane over an upland farmscape.

From the Icknield Way Association information board (see above), the route heads north-east along the edge of the golf course. Over a cross-tracks, where the golf course ends, it keeps ahead to a second cross-tracks, where the deer logo waymarks indicate that the route has crossed into Hertfordshire. From here the route is described in the next pub walk.

[7] **Lilley** (Hertfordshire)
The Lilley Arms

Lilley is an attractive 'estate' village and many of the thatched cottages bear a lion rampant crest.

Originally built as a coaching inn, much of the old character of the Lilley Arms has survived, together with its long tradition of offering hospitality to travellers by providing bed and breakfast accommodation. As a hostelry 'worth passing a few pubs for', it has two separate, comfortably furnished bars in which to enjoy real ale and home cooking. The ham and sausages are prepared locally and very free-range eggs are provided by the chickens that wander the courtyard behind the pub. Steak and kidney pie cooked in Abbot Ale is an all-time favourite, whilst hot salt-beef sandwiches of generous proportions provide a meal in themselves. Traditional Sunday lunches are so popular it is advisable to book in advance. Children's portions are available and there is always a choice of vegetarian dishes. Meals are not served on Sunday nights. There is a pleasant garden and courtyard to the rear of the pub where the more adventurous are free to mingle with a variety of 'rescued' animals, including the numerous farmyard fowls, goats, a sheep and a Vietnamese pot-bellied pig. Less hardy spirits might try the small barn in the corner where 'bits and bobs' and rural 'bygones' are on sale.

The Lilley Arms is a Greene King pub and serves their IPA and Abbot Ale. Guinness, lager and cider are also available on draught.

The opening times are Monday to Friday from 11.30 am to 3 pm and 5.30 pm to 11 pm. On Saturday the hours are from 11.30 am to 11 pm, and on Sunday from noon to 10.30 pm.

Telephone: 01462 768371.

How to get there: Lilley lies 2 miles north-east of Luton. The village can be reached by following minor roads from the A6 at Streatley, or from the A505 (Luton to Hitchin). The pub is on a no-through-road in the centre of the village, near the church.

Parking: There is limited parking in a small courtyard to the rear of the pub, or roadside parking in front.

Length of the walk: 5½ miles (short-cuts available). Map: OS Landranger 166 Luton, Hertford and surrounding area (inn GR 118265).

A walk across a lovely, rolling, upland farmscape with wide views, especially from Telegraph Hill.

The Walk

From the pub the walk turns left, along the no-through-road. Past a thatched cottage on the right, the road continues as a wide and often rutted track. The walk follows the track ahead where a farm road comes in from the right, after which the track bears left, then right, around the edge of Ward's Wood. Along this stretch there are wide views across open farmland and in the spring the wood is full of primroses and bluebells. Over a rise the track runs down to a cross-tracks, where the walk turns right along a field-edge track with good views of nearby Galley Hill, until, eventually, another major cross-tracks is reached.

Here, the route turns right, along the Icknield Way Path. Within a short distance the track runs under the National Grid and continues to a metal gate next to a road. Through a gap past the end of a gate, the walk follows the road ahead, which runs down to Treasures Grove Picnic Site. Through a small car park, a short-cut can be taken by turning right, along a field-edge path (see sketch map).

The main walk, however, keeps ahead along a field edge track to the corner, from where it goes straight on, through woods. Just past two magnificent, mature beech trees the track reaches a Y-junction, in the middle of which an information board gives details of the wildlife in this important, chalk grassland nature reserve. Here, a second short-cut follows the track to the right (see sketch map).

The main walk bears right and ahead as it climbs fairly steeply to the top

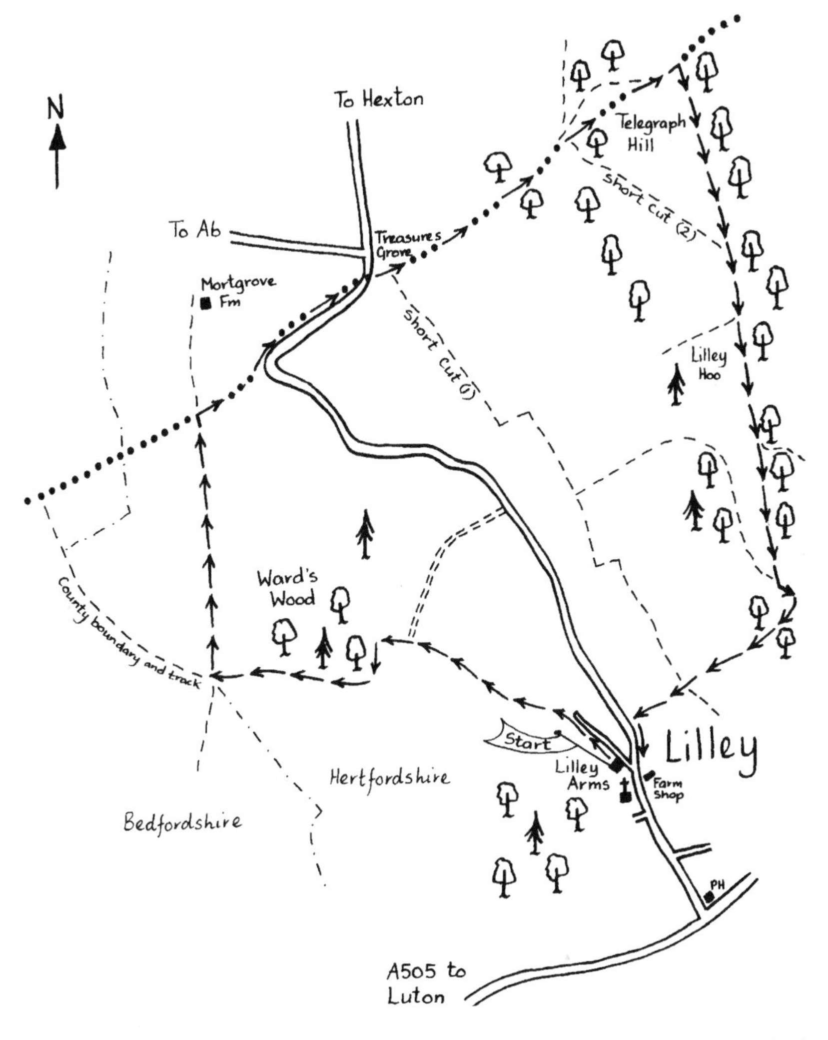

of Telegraph Hill, named after the wooden semaphore signal station which once stood here. From this high ground there are extensive views to the north across the Bedfordshire plain. Over the rise, the walk follows a field-edge path down to the corner of another arable field, where the Icknield Way Path bears left and ahead on a broad track, but the pub walk turns right, on a bridleway.

On the other side of a small wood it follows a track across wide, arable fields that used to be open downland. Known as Lilley Hoo, in the 17th century a racecourse was established on this flat area and meetings were popular social occasions in the county. Today, the whole plateau is covered by a sea of cereal crops in which some of the ancient trackways have sunk out of sight.

At the corner of a hedgerow the main walk is joined by the second short-cut coming in from the right. From here the walk keeps ahead along a track and hedge which, eventually, passes under the National Grid. Ignoring the permissive path to the right, it continues ahead on the track which keeps to the right-hand side of a wood, beyond which this section of the track is permissive. Just past the tree line in the corner, the walk bears left, along another track. After about 50 yards, it turns sharply right, at a way-marked post, to follow a footpath through the trees. Emerging at a small clearing, it bears left on a path that descends steeply into the valley, with views of Lilley below.

At the bottom, the walk continues ahead at a junction where the first short-cut comes in from the right. From here a hedged track runs up to join a drive which is followed to the road. Here, the walk turns left, and follows the road through the village. Just before the village farm shop is reached (well worth a visit for its range of home-made jams and local produce), the walk turns right, along the no-through-road, back to the pub.

Icknield Way Path – Hertfordshire border to Pirton (3½ miles)

For the route from the Hertfordshire border to Telegraph Hill, see above. This short stretch follows a track off which paths on the left lead to the top of nearby Deacon Hill, a detour worth making for the panoramic views.

From Telegraph Hill, the track runs ahead, slightly downhill, and eventually meets the B655. Here, the route turns right for a short distance, before turning left, to follow a field-edge bridleway signposted to Pirton. From here the route is described in the next pub walk.

[8] **Pirton** (Hertfordshire)
The Cat and Fiddle

Pirton is a small, rural village with a lot to offer for its size, including a village green, an ancient church, a motte and bailey mound and the choice of three pubs!

Built 100 or so years ago and facing onto the green, the Cat and Fiddle is itself an example of the way in which good things come in small packages! For small it is, with one bar divided by an arch into two snug and cosy areas with open fireplaces at each end. Popular with both locals and walkers, the pub serves traditional bar meals, including home-made pies, scampi and chips, chilli con carne and chicken curry. The establishment's popularity means that there is no room for children inside and groups or parties are advised to telephone in advance. However, picnic-style tables on the village green and in the very pleasant garden to the rear provide the perfect setting for alfresco summer meals.

The Cat and Fiddle is a freehouse and cask ales on offer include Boddingtons Bitter, as well as Charles Wells Fargo and Eagle IPA. Guinness, cider and lager are available on draught.

The pub is closed at lunchtimes on Monday and on this day opens from 4 pm to 11 pm only. On Tuesday to Saturday it opens from noon to 11 pm, and on Sunday from noon to 10.30 pm.

Telephone: 01462 712245.

How to get there: Pirton is just 2 miles north-west of Hitchin between the A6 (Bedford to Luton) and the A600 (Bedford to Hitchin). Turn off the B655 between Barton-le-Clay and Hitchin to follow minor roads. The pub is on the green on the southern side of the village.

Parking: There are spaces on the road in front of the pub, or round the village green.

Length of the walk: 4 miles (short-cut available). Map: OS Landranger 166 Luton, Hertford and surrounding area (inn GR 145315).

A pleasant walk, with good views from the high ground to the south and west of the village.

The Walk

From the pub the walk follows the Icknield Way Path as it bears left, over the village green, and past the Motte and Bailey public house. About 100 yards down Crabtree Lane it turns right, on a path leading to the church, which adjoins the site of a 12th-century Norman castle. Steps lead to the top of the mound known as Toot [lookout] Hill with what is left of the encircling moat below. The church, St Mary's, is worth visiting for the serenity of its largely unadorned interior which, luckily, escaped over-restoration in the Victorian era.

Past the gate to the church, the walk turns left, through a swing-gate at the base of the mound. From here it parts company with the Icknield Way Path as it bears right, across a pasture in which bumps and hollows may indicate extended earthworks and fortifications in Norman times. Through another swing-gate opposite a half-timbered, red-brick barn, it turns right, along a lane. At the T-junction the walk crosses the road to follow a footpath signposted 'Old Wellbury'. The path runs uphill, across arable fields, before meeting a track, along which the walk turns left. At a T-junction of tracks it turns right, then almost immediately left, over a stile on the edge of rough pasture. From the stile the walk keeps more or less ahead, over the rise and past High Down House, an impressive building with a stone arch leading to an inner courtyard. Legend has it that on the anniversary of his murder by Cromwell's Roundheads the headless ghost of a Cavalier rides out of the house and across the fields, seeking sanctuary in nearby Hitchin Priory.

Past the house the walk bears slightly left, to the far left-hand corner of the field. Here, a path to the right, along the edge of the wood, provides a short-cut (see sketch map). The main walk, however, goes over the stile and then keeps to the left of a hedge down and up again across open pasture. In the corner it climbs a steep bank to a busy road (the B655), along which the walk turns left. After a short distance it turns off the road, on a footpath

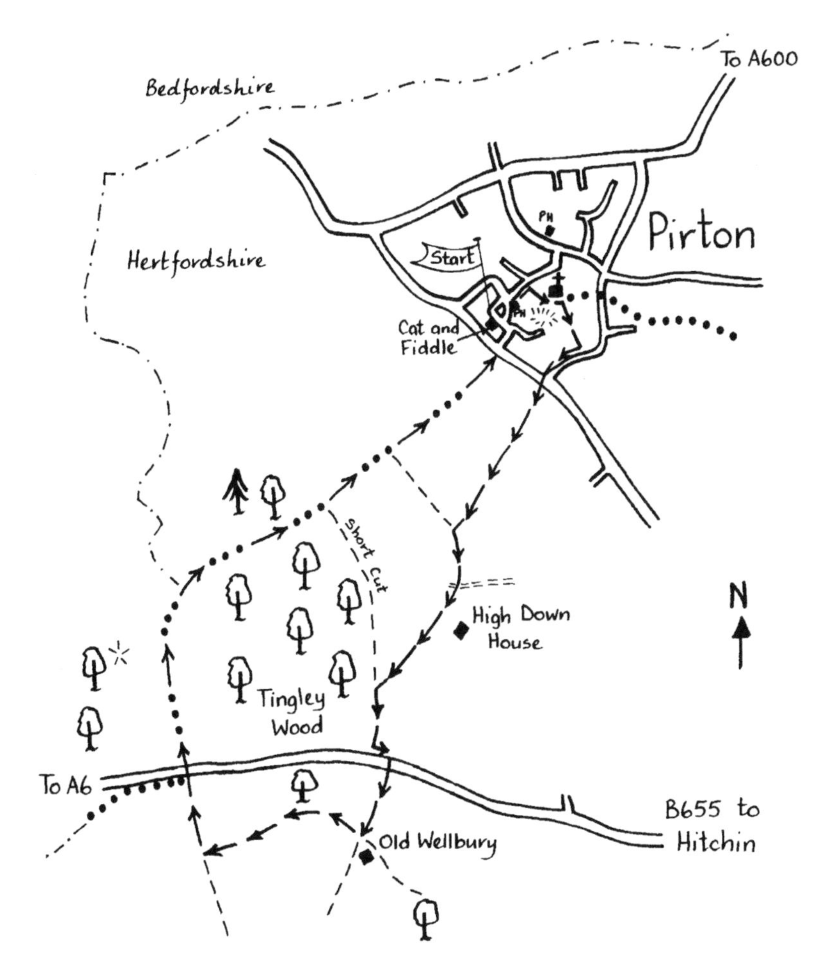

to the right. From here the walk follows a field-edge path and hedge to the top of the rise, where it turns right and, almost immediately, right again, on a path heading diagonally across an arable field. On the far side of the field the walk bears left, along the hedge, to the corner. Through the hedge it keeps ahead across another wide, arable field with Deacon Hill prominent in front. Eventually, a farm road is reached, along which the route turns right, back down to the road crossed earlier.

Keeping ahead across the road, the walk joins the Icknield Way Path, which follows a field-edge bridleway. At the far end of the field the woods on the other side conceal an ancient barrow or burial mound, one of many to be found along the line of the hills. Past a mature beech tree, the walk turns right, in the top corner, to follow a good downhill track.

This is hedged in at first but, eventually, it opens up on the right-hand side to provide fine views across rolling fields and woods – made all the more enjoyable by easy walking on a grassy track shaded by fine beeches.

After a good distance the short-cut comes in from the right and the track keeps ahead before, eventually, meeting a road on the fringes of Pirton. Here, the walk crosses over to follow the road ahead, which leads back to the village green and the pub.

Icknield Way Path – Pirton to Ickleford (3 miles)

For the route from the B655 to Pirton, see above.

This section provides easy walking across a flat, arable farmscape.

Past the Motte and Bailey pub, the route turns right, on a path leading to the church. In front of the mound next to the church, it crosses a small pasture to another road, which is dog-legged across, right, then left. Clear of the houses and a playing field, it follows a track which leads for a good mile across arable fields before turning right, along a green lane to a white cottage.

Here, the route turns left, and follows a lane through the outskirts of Ickleford. Keeping ahead over the A600, it follows Turnpike Lane to a T-junction at the centre of the village, where it turns left, past two pubs. Opposite the church it turns right, on a track. From here the route is described in the next pub walk.

[9] **Ickleford** (Hertfordshire)

The Cricketers

Ickleford has an ancient church and four pubs. At the centre of the village stand two of them, adjoining, one of which is said to have been connected with the nearby church by underground passages.

The Cricketers, a short distance further along the road, has been much altered over the centuries, having served as a house, a shop and a dairy before conversion to its present use. Originally known as the Live and Let Live, its current name relates to a time when two prominent members of the village cricket team lived in the pub. Today, the cricketing tradition is proudly maintained and the inn fields no less than three cricket teams. The pleasant open-plan interior is divided into nooks, crannies and levels which reflect the various uses to which the building has been put. Tables and stools are supplemented by settles converted from chapel pews, whilst an eye-catching collection of over 200 water jugs hangs from wooden beams. Bar meals range from enormous sandwiches the size of a carthorse's hoof (known as Huffers) to home-baked ham, egg and chips. Daily 'specials' include such dishes as steak and ale pie and a range of balti curries. There is a vegetarian choice and children's portions are available. Meals are not served on a Sunday night. There is a small garden to the rear of the pub, where dogs are welcome.

The Cricketers is a freehouse and prides itself on the very wide range of real ales on offer – indeed, CAMRA likens a visit to the pub to a 'brewery trip round England'! There are eight handpumps in all, three of which generally serve Tetley Bitter, Ruddles Best and Bass. On the others you may find, for example, Shepherd Neame Best Bitter, Mildmay Brewery SP, Mitchells and Butlers Brew XI, Hall and Woodhouse Tanglefoot, and Webster's Green Label. The real ales change on an almost daily basis, and over 20 'reinforcements' await their turn in the cellar. Guinness, Simmonds Bitter, cider and lager are also available on draught.

The opening times are Monday to Friday from 11 am to 3 pm and from 6 pm to 11 pm. On Saturday the hours are from 11 am to 11 pm, and on Sunday from noon to 10.30 pm.

Telephone: 01462 432629.

How to get there: Ickleford is only 1 mile north of Hitchin and 2 miles west of Letchworth. Turn off the A600 (Hitchin to Bedford). The pub is on the northern outskirts of the village, on the road to Letchworth.

Parking: There is a large car park to the rear of the pub.

Length of the walk: 3 miles (short-cut available). Map: OS Landranger 166 Luton, Hertford and surrounding area (inn GR 185322).

A walk via 'Gerry's Hole' up to Wilbury Hill, with good views over the surrounding countryside.

The Walk

From the pub the walk turns right, along the road. Just before the church on the right is reached, the walk crosses over the road and turns left, along the waymarked Icknield Way Path.

From a metal gate the path continues to a bridge and footbridge over the river Hiz, over which a track is followed to Gerry's Hole, a small pond on the right. Here an information board gives details of Gerry's fate which, in Victorian times, would have served as a 'cautionary tale' and 'dreadful warning' to all those of intemperate habits. As a navvy he worked with pick and shovel building the nearby railway line. At the end of a particularly hard and thirsty day's work, he drank too much of the local ale, fell into this pond on his way home and drowned – pub walkers, beware!

Past the pond, a hedged track leads to the main railway line, which must be crossed with care as express trains travel along this stretch of track at more than 100 mph. Over the railway, a path leads through bushes and along a chain-link boundary fence. Where the fence ends, the walk stays with the track ahead across open farmland, with Wilbury Hill on the skyline in front. At a T-junction next to a wooden bench seat, a track turning left provides a short-cut which avoids climbing the hill (see sketch map).

The main walk, however, stays ahead on the track climbing up Wilbury Hill. At the top the Icknield Way Path crosses straight over the road, while the pub walk turns left, just before the road is reached. From here it follows the path through Wilbury Hill picnic site, on the other side of which it turns left again, just short of the Wilbury public house. At a way-marked post the Icknield Way Riders' Route turns left, but the pub walk follows the track ahead. Past the end of a small wood and a wooden bench seat, the walk follows the track as it forks left at a junction. From here the track is followed downhill and through a farmyard to a T-junction, opposite some stables. Here, the short-cut comes in from the left and rejoins the main walk, which turns right, along to the nearby road.

At the road the route turns left, and follows the road under a railway bridge, on the other side of which it crosses over the river Hiz for the second time. Just past the river the walk turns left, at a fingerpost, and follows a footpath which runs more or less parallel with the road, back to the pub.

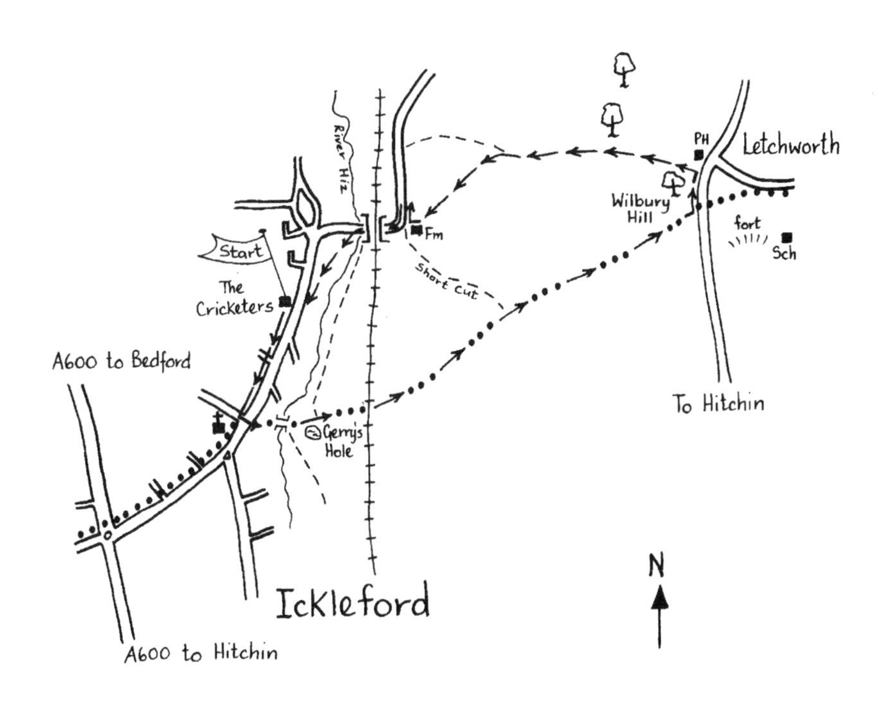

Icknield Way Path – Ickleford to Baldock (5 miles)

For the route from Ickleford to Wilbury Hill, see above. This link passes through the built-up area between Letchworth and Baldock.

From Wilbury Hill the route crosses the road and continues ahead on a field-edge path. At the corner it turns left, to Icknield Way Road, down which it turns right. After about ½ mile, it turns right, along Spring Road, and left, just before a railway bridge, along a path following the embankment. Eventually, steps lead up to the road where the route turns left, in front of the Spirella factory. (Letchworth's main shopping centre from which there is a frequent bus service to Baldock is to the right.) Opposite Spirella, the route turns right, along Nevells Road, then left, down the Quadrant. Over the road and onto Norton Common, it turns right, on a tarmac path running parallel to the main road. Past the open-air swimming pool it turns right, up to and across the junction to follow Icknield Way East. At a T-junction it turns left, on Green Lane, then right, along Blackhorse Road. Over the rise, it runs down to and, right, along Knapp Close, at the end of which a path leads over the railway, then a field to a footbridge across the A1(M).

From here, the route follows the road ahead to a T-junction, where the walk turns left, then right, down Pond Lane. At the end it turns right, along Church Street, past St Mary's church to the crossroads at the centre of Baldock. From here the route is described in the next pub walk.

[10] **Baldock** (Hertfordshire)

The Rose and Crown Hotel

Baldock grew to prosperity as a market town and important staging post on the old Great North Road from York to London. Today, many attractive buildings still line its broad High Street, close to one end of which is the Rose and Crown.

Originally built as a coaching inn, the hotel carries on a long tradition of hospitality for travellers, and these days provides stylish comfort with a spacious bar room and adjoining restaurant. There is a good selection of typical bar meals, including baked potatoes with a variety of fillings, whilst the restaurant menu offers home-made pies, such as beef and Guinness, or a range of 'speciality' steaks. There is a choice for vegetarians and meals are served throughout the week. Children are welcome in the restaurant. Dogs are not allowed inside, but there is a patio area in the yard to the rear.

The Rose and Crown is a Greene King establishment and serves their IPA and Abbot Ale, plus a seasonal real ale. Guinness, Murphy's, lager and cider are also available on draught.

The opening times are Monday to Saturday from 11 am to 11 pm, and on Sunday from noon to 10.30 pm.

Telephone: 01462 892339.

How to get there: Baldock is on the eastern side of the A1(M), adjoining Letchworth. The A505 (Hitchin to Royston) and the A507 (Shefford to Buntingford) meet at the centre of the town. The pub is on Whitehorse Street, next to the crossroads at the northern end of the High Street.

Parking: There is ample parking along one side of the High Street.

Length of the walk: 6½ miles (short-cut available). Map: OS Landranger 166 Luton, Hertford and surrounding area (inn GR 246339).

A walk with wonderful views en route to Wallington, where George Orwell was married whilst living in the village.

The Walk

From the pub the walk turns left, then left again at the crossroads. Now in company with the Icknield Way Path, the walk turns left at the roundabout at the end of the High Street. After a short distance it turns right, along Limekiln Lane. Past the mobile homes site, it follows a path to open fields where the walk continues ahead on a field-edge track for well over a mile. Beyond farm buildings and over a cross-tracks it follows a footpath across a wide, arable field, on the far side of which it turns left, on a field-edge path to the A507. Over the road, it follows a grassy track up and over the hill in front before crossing a narrow lane. Here, a short-cut can be taken by turning left (see sketch map).

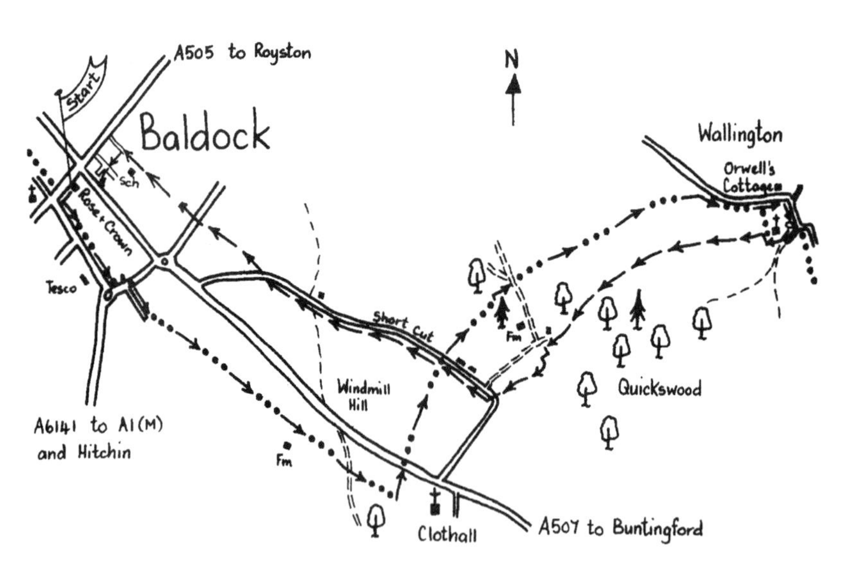

The main walk, however, continues ahead for some distance before bearing left, then right, on a track through trees. Past a barn, it crosses over a track and keeps more or less ahead, following grassy tracks across high ground with good views across open countryside to the north. At a road the route turns right and, at the top of the rise, the Icknield Way Path turns off to the right. The pub walk, however, follows the road, which runs down into Wallington. On the left-hand side of the sharp bend to the right is the white, thatched cottage where George Orwell lived from 1936–1940. The road runs up to a T-junction next to a duck pond, where the walk turns right, to St Mary's church. Here, George Orwell was married and facsimiles of the marriage certificate are on sale in the church, together with postcards of the cottage in which he lived.

Past the church, the walk turns right, along a track for about 100 yards, then left, over a stile. From here the walk follows a path over a footbridge in the middle of a field and then across stiles each side of a small meadow. The path leads just inside a small wood to a clearing where the walk bears left, along the edge of another wood. Where the wood ends the walk turns left, along a drive leading away from a cottage in front of which stands a horse-drawn gypsy caravan.

Just before reaching the front of a magnificent farmhouse, the walk turns left, along a hedge and ditch. Within a few yards it crosses over a footbridge and turns left, along a field-edge path. At the corner it turns right, then almost immediately left, along a narrow path leading to a lane. Here, the route turns right, past the entrance to Quickswood Farm, and follows the lane up to and past a line of cottages beyond which it crosses back over the line of the outward route. This time the walk stays with the lane, which runs downhill for a good mile. Past a large barn on the right, just as the lane bends left, the walk keeps ahead on a footpath across fields to a road on the outskirts of Baldock.

Over the road, it follows a cycle-track and, past Hartsfield School, turns left, on a path to the left of a line of garages. Where the path meets a road, the walk crosses over to run down a cul-de-sac, at the end of which it turns left, on a path leading to the main road. Here, the walk turns right, to a crossroads, where it turns left, back to the Rose and Crown.

Icknield Way Path – Baldock to Therfield (10 miles)

For the route from Baldock to Wallington, see above.

Between Baldock and Royston the traditional Icknield Way is now a busy main road, therefore the Icknield Way Path now mainly follows sunken green lanes, which can be muddy in wet weather.

Just before Wallington, the route turns right, on a bridleway, then left, along a lane past a church. At the road junction it turns right, over a stile and across a meadow to another stile to the left of silos. At the far corner of another field it dog-legs across a farm track and runs downhill to a culvert across a stream. From here it takes the left of three paths across a field, aiming to the left of cottages on the outskirts of Redhill.

At the road it turns left, then right, along a track, at the end of which it follows a path and a hedge through which it turns left, over a footbridge and stile. From here it crosses a small pasture and, past the house with solar panels, arrives at Roe Green.

Bearing right across the road, the route runs to a stile behind a small pond, from where it angles right, over several paddocks and stiles, back to the road. Here, it turns left, past the Chequers public house and into Sandon, before bearing right, up to the village green. Through the lych gate, the route follows a path from the rear of All Saints' church to the Therfield road. Here, it turns right and follows the road as far as a bend, where it turns right, on Park Lane, a byway track. After bearing right, the track winds through trees before meeting, and turning left along, another road.

At a T-junction it turns left, then left again, along a drive to a house before which it forks right, along another byway track, known as Notley Lane. At another T-junction it turns right and, eventually, left over a new, wooden bridge. From here the track leads up to drier ground where the route turns right on a farm road. Where the road bends left, the route keeps ahead on another byway track for some distance before turning left, over a stile next to a gate. From here a path heads diagonally right, over several fields to a road, along which the route turns left, into the village of Therfield. From the village green, the route is described in the next pub walk.

[11] **Therfield** (Hertfordshire)
The Fox and Duck

Therfield is not far from Royston, which has a museum and a unique, man-made cave, open to visitors throughout the summer.

The Fox and Duck faces the village green and is an all too rare example of a 'born again' pub! Once closed, but now refurbished both inside and out, it has re-opened for business to the vast relief of all concerned – for it's a poor thing, a village that has lost its pub . . . Inside the Victorian, red-brick building, wooden settles and a flagstone floor create a country style. Past the end of the long, L-shaped bar is a very comfortably furnished restaurant serving such dishes as home-made soups and pies, grilled steaks, or the house speciality – confit of Barbary duck with stir-fry vegetables. Traditional Sunday lunches plus home-made puds make this inn especially popular at weekends. There is a vegetarian menu and meals are served throughout the week. Children are welcome in the restaurant and have their own play area in the large garden behind the building. Dogs are not allowed inside.

The Fox and Duck is a freehouse and serves Ruddles Best, Wadworth 6X, Courage Directors, Old Speckled Hen and John Smith's Bitter. Guinness,

Beamish Stout, lager and cider are also available on draught.

The opening times are Monday to Friday from 11.30 am to 3 pm and 6 pm to 11 pm. On Saturday the hours are from 11.30 am to 11 pm, and on Sunday from noon to 10.30 pm.

Telephone: 01763 287246.

How to get there: Therfield lies between the A505 and the A10(T), just 2 miles south-west of Royston. The village is well signposted off either the A505 or the A10. The pub is at the centre, to one side of the village green.

Parking: There is a car park behind the pub.

Length of the walk: 6½ miles (short-cut available). Map: OS Landranger 154 Cambridge, Newmarket and surrounding area (inn GR 336373).

Each leg of this walk reveals its own views and has its own special interest, from open farmland to heathland, from golf courses to horse gallops, from ancient barrows to nature reserves.

The Walk

The walk follows the Icknield Way Path up the right-hand side of the pub. Clear of the buildings, it goes over a field to a footbridge, from where it crosses the corner of another field to a gap in the hedge. Here it bears right, on a track heading east, which dips down before continuing ahead across open countryside for about a mile. Eventually, where the track bends sharply right, the walk follows a footpath which continues ahead to a metal stile next to a gate. Over the stile the path leads to the top end of Therfield Heath, one of the richest areas of chalk grassland in East Anglia.

Wide views open up across the heath as the walk bears left, on a path down the length of a small combe and one-time rifle range. Further on, the path keeps to the right of a rugby pitch before arriving at the Therfield Heath Sporting Club. Here, information boards give full details of the heath and its history, whilst a cafe/bar, open to the public, provides the opportunity for a halfway break!

From here the Icknield Way Path continues down to the road and turns right, through Royston. The pub walk, however, turns left and goes through the car park above the clubhouse before heading uphill, aiming for a mound surmounted by a memorial seat. Past the seat, the walk continues uphill, across the upper half of a golf course whose sixteenth hole is known locally as Cardiac Hill! Panoramic views to the north extend well beyond Cambridge on a fine day whilst nearby, on the fairway, is a rare example of a Neolithic long barrow which itself makes a good viewing point for a cluster of Bronze Age round barrows.

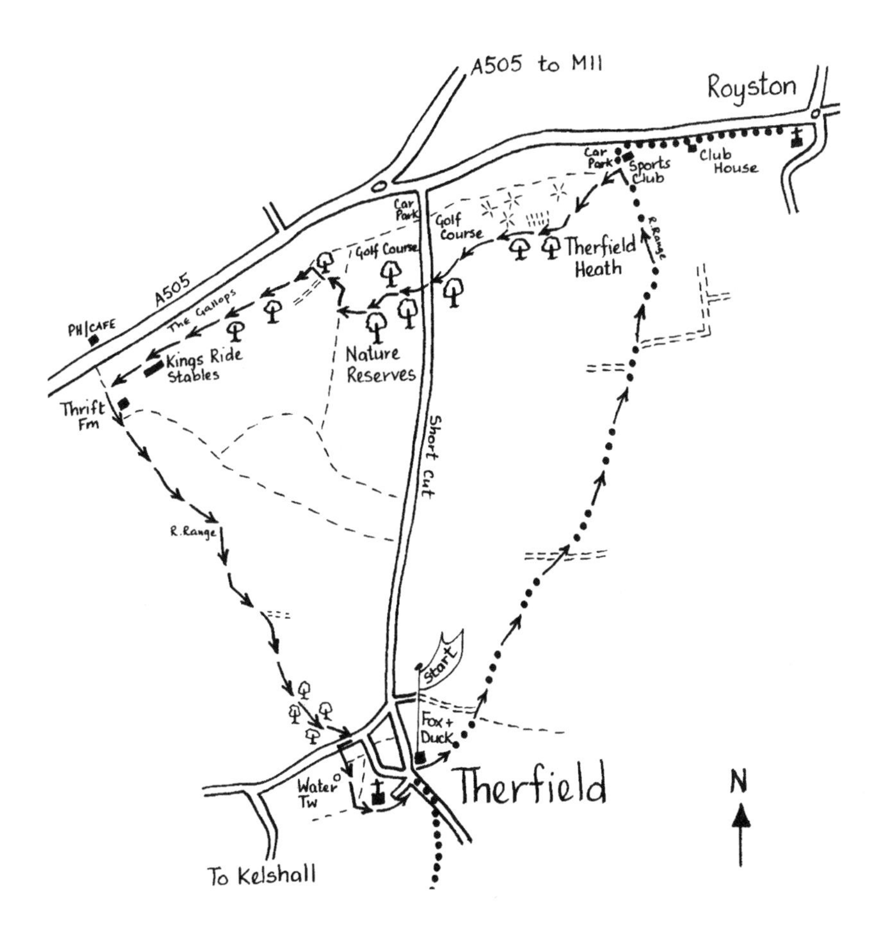

At the tree line the walk bears right, along the upper edge of the golf course. At a corner to the left of a green it follows a path under the boughs of overhanging beech trees to a gravelled path. Here, it turns left, and follows the path round to the right before turning left, through trees and down to a road. At this point a short-cut can be taken by turning left and following the road for over a mile, back to the pub (see sketch map).

The main walk, however, crosses straight over the road and follows a path which leads ahead through two nature reserves in which pathside information boards give details of local wildlife. After passing through Fox Covert Nature Reserve, the track bears left, through the beeches, then right, to emerge back in the open. From here the walk runs along the top of a mini-ridge and down to a track, along which it turns right. At the next junction it turns left, on a track which bears away from this end of the golf course to an open gateway. Without going through the gate, the walk turns right and follows the fence to a high hedge through which it turns left, along the hedge-line. Below, to the right, are the horse gallops used to train racehorses from local stables which, in recent years, have been winners of many races, including the Derby, Grand National and Cesarewitch.

After about ½ mile King's Ride racehorse stables are passed on the left and the walk turns left, on a farm road through the yard of Thrift Farm. Past the barns, it follows a good track across wide fields, aiming for the distant water tower on the ridge ahead. Where the track turns left, the walk continues ahead on a field-edge path past a small rifle range. Over a track, a fingerpost indicates the Therfield path which leads up to the corner of a wide, arable field. From here the sunken path climbs to meet a road on the top of the wooded ridge along which the walk turns right, for about 50 yards, then left, along a track. Past an ancient, thatched, manor house on the left, it passes the water tower seen earlier in the walk as a distant landmark. At St Mary's church it turns left, through the churchyard, to join a narrow lane leading to a road along which the walk again turns left. Within a short distance the road runs up to the village green, opposite the pub.

Icknield Way Path – Therfield to Heydon (8 miles)

For the route from Therfield to Therfield Heath (Royston), see above. After passing through the centre of Royston, a town with many attractions for the visitor, the route again follows mainly green lanes across upland countryside.

Having turned right on the edge of Therfield Heath, the old A505 is followed through Royston and ahead, over the roundabout. From here it follows the roadside path uphill. Where the path ends it crosses over to the right, along a drive for about 50 yards before turning left, on a path through beech trees. Clear of the trees, it follows a field-edge path downhill, which runs parallel to the main road for about a mile before turning right, along a waymarked farm road. Past several houses on the left, it keeps ahead on this track for over a mile and crosses into Cambridgeshire. Over the B1368 it continues ahead and crosses a small lane to follow a track to the right of a ditch, keeping ahead where a track comes in from the right. From here the route is described in the next pub walk.

[12] **Heydon** (Cambridgeshire)
The King William IV

Heydon is an attractive village and home to the Wood Green Animal Shelter. The King William IV stands by the side of the road almost next door.

The pub dates back to the 17th century and, apart from the building, its new owners acquired the contents of a truly amazing interior which really does have to be seen to be believed! Every nook and cranny has been crammed with an amazing profusion of bygones and memorabilia. A salvaged, stucco panel adds to the monumental effect of the long bar. To the rear, a copper font dominates a riotous assembly of bits and pieces, including clocks, giant bellows, lamps, pots, pans, china and rural implements. A huge, double sided, open fireplace separates this from the front, where a statue of St Joseph presides over more of the same and the 'ostlers restaurant', its walls festooned with harness. Given that the bar tables are suspended on chains from beams in the ceiling, the overall effect is probably best described as tongue-in-cheek, mock gothic, or camp, Hammer Horror! Even so, comfort has not been sacrificed in the name of unconventionality as all the built-in furniture is luxuriously upholstered. The restaurant serves a good range of bar meals and snacks, including ploughman's, pies and jacket potatoes. The à la carte menu includes dishes such as grilled rainbow trout almondine, mushroom and broccoli mornay, and king sized vol-au-vent filled with stir fried vegetables, and there is always a vegetarian selection. Children are welcome in the dining area, and meals are available throughout the week. Well-behaved dogs are allowed in the bars if kept on a lead, and there is a very pleasant garden to the rear of the pub.

The King William IV is a freehouse and serves Draught Bass, Worthington Best Bitter, Greene King IPA, and Morland Old Speckled Hen. A choice of guest real ales depends on the season. Caffrey's Bitter, Beamish Stout, lager and cider are also available on draught.

The opening times are Monday to Saturday from 11 am to 3 pm and 6 pm to 11 pm, and on Sunday from noon to 10.30 pm.

Telephone: 01763 838773.

How to get there: Heydon lies 4 miles east of Royston, but just in Cambridgeshire, between the A505 and the B1039. Turn off either and follow minor roads. The pub is on the Great Chishill road on the southern edge of the village.

Parking: There is a large car park to the rear of the pub.

Length of the walk: 4½ miles. Map: OS Landranger 154 Cambridge, Newmarket and surrounding area (inn GR 432397).

Wonderful views unfold on this walk from Heydon, one of the highest villages in Cambridgeshire. At the start there is also an opportunity to visit Wood Green Animal Shelter.

The Walk

From the pub the walk turns left, and follows the road past the post office and Wood Green Animal Shelter, open until 3 pm throughout the week. From the Shelter it continues along the road, which now runs through the remnants of apple orchards that once stretched all the way from here to Saffron Walden. Past the village sign for Great Chishill (where there is a restored post mill open to the public from April to October – see sketch map), the walk turns right, along a footpath to the left of a pink-washed, thatched cottage.

The path runs down the side of an orchard to the right and, further along, a wood on the left. It keeps ahead where a path turns off left, and emerges in the corner of a vast, arable field with wide views across rolling farmland to the north-west. From here the walk follows the path ahead, which keeps to the left of a hedge as it runs up and over a rise. Where the hedge ends, the view extends to a hill on the right on which can be seen the remains of the artificial terraces cut into the slope in medieval times to form platforms for cultivation, known as a 'strip lynchets'.

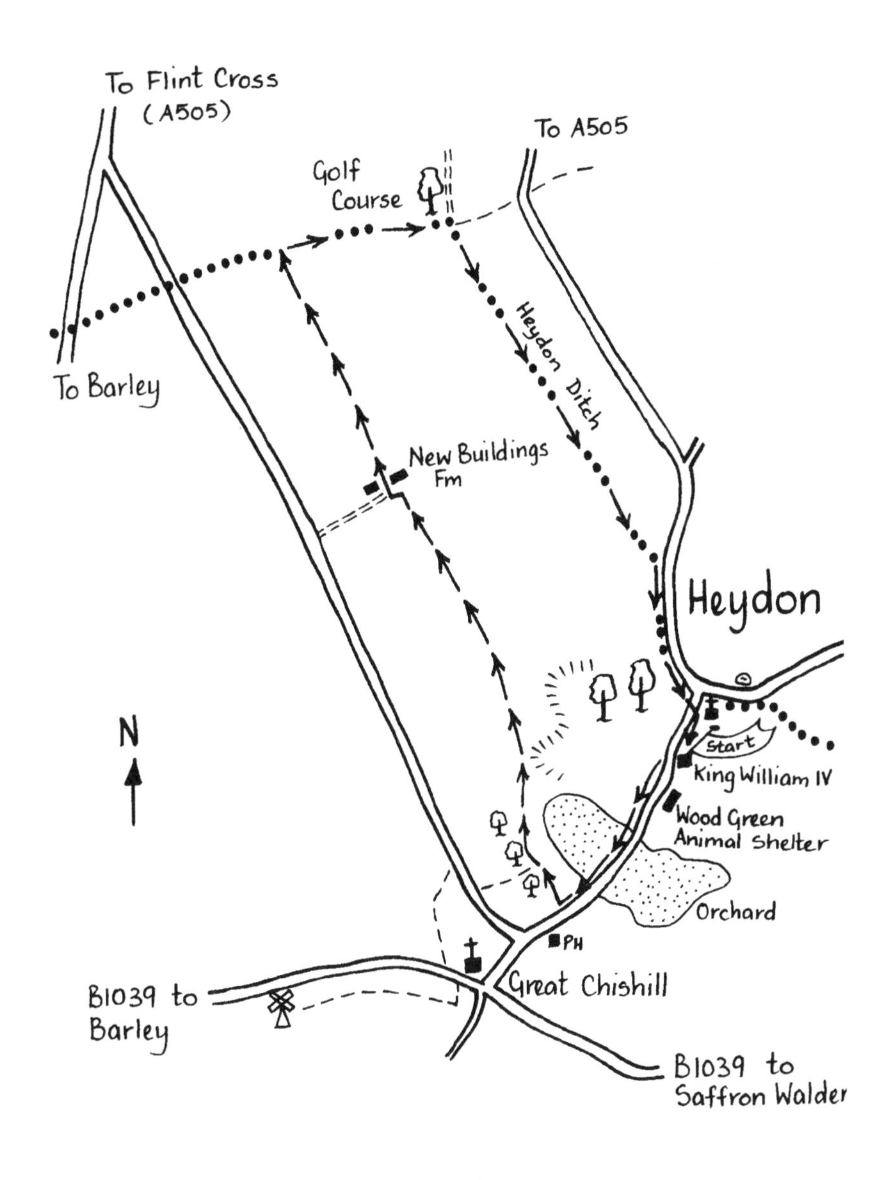

The path keeps ahead along the line of electricity poles between two prairie-sized fields, on the other side of which is New Buildings Farm, an island in a sea of cereal crops. Here, the walk dog-legs left, then right, to follow a good track past a terraced row of farm cottages. Clear of the farm buildings, it continues to head north-west.

Views ahead extend as far as Duxford, a famous RAF fighter station during World War II and the base from which Douglas Bader's squadron played a leading role in 'Big Wing' operations during the Battle of Britain. Today, it is home to the Imperial War Museum's collection of over 100 military aircraft, many of which are still airworthy. Rolls-Royce Merlins still sing their distinctive song on flying-display days and, in this part of East Anglia, it is always worth keeping an eye on the sky for unusual 'types' on test flights.

Eventually, the track leads down to a T-junction in front of a golf course, where the walk joins the Icknield Way Path as it turns right, along a hedged green lane. At the next cross-tracks, to the right of a small wood, the walk turns right, along a track known as Heydon Ditch. This track runs between wide, arable fields for a good ½ mile before climbing back up the ridge ahead, from the top of which there are more wide views to the north and west. From the top corner a path bears left to the road, along which the walk turns right.

The road is followed up through the village of Heydon, which has fine examples of flint-knapped walls and thatched cottages. At the top of the rise, where the road forks, stands Holy Trinity church, its tower rebuilt with red bricks as a result of wartime bomb damage. Here, the Icknield Way Path turns left, but the pub walk turns right and follows the road which leads back to the pub.

Icknield Way Path – from before Heydon Ditch to Elmdon (2 miles)

For the route from Heydon Ditch to Heydon village, see above.

The next part of the walk is a short stretch from Heydon, one of the highest villages in Cambridgeshire, with good views as the route crosses arable farmland into Essex.

At the road junction in front of the bus shelter, the route follows the road left, round to a pond, opposite which it turns right, along a waymarked track. After bending left, then right (good views to the north of Duxford Airfield, Europe's top aviation museum), a path is followed ahead across an arable field, on the other side of which it turns left. Over a footbridge on the right (into Essex), it leads to a narrow lane. Here, the route turns right and, past an old pump on the left, it turns left opposite a thatched cottage. From here a path runs diagonally left over a small pasture to another lane, along which it turns right into Chrishall. At a crossroads, with the Red Cow to the right, the route crosses over left, and runs through a transport garage yard. From here the route is described in the next pub walk.

[13] **Elmdon** (Essex)
The King's Head

The wool trade brought prosperity to Elmdon and the King's Head was originally built in the 1600s as a storehouse for fleeces. Various extensions over the centuries have resulted in a building of much character, including a Grade I listed games room! It stands next to an ex-pub, the Carrier, which still has its original wooden sign and Greene King wall plaque. The King's Head, however, is alive, well and very active in the local community. The village church stands opposite, which may, or may not, have something to do with the inscription on an old church pew inside the pub which says, 'It is better to sit in a pub and think of a church than sit in a church and think of a pub'!

Accommodation is based on the traditional arrangement of two separate bars, one of which incorporates a dining area. Brass lamps, copper plates and pans, carpenters' tools and agricultural implements adorn the walls and create a rural atmosphere. Honest, home-cooked pub grub using fresh, local produce includes fish from the trout farm, steak and kidney pies for the traditionalists, and beef curry for the more adventurous. Children are welcome in the eating section. There is a very attractive garden behind the pub with an extensive pets' corner of rescued animals and birds presided over by Wilbur, a Vietnamese pot-bellied pig. Bed and breakfast accommodation is available, although it is advisable to book in advance.

The King's Head is an Ind Coope house serving Tetley Bitter and Greene King IPA. Guinness, cider and lager are on draught.

The opening times are Monday to Friday from 12 noon to 2.30 pm and 6 pm to 11 pm. On Saturday the hours are from 12 noon to 11 pm and on Sunday from 12 noon to 10.30 pm.

Telephone: 01763 838358.

How to get there: Elmdon is 2 miles west of the M11 in the north-west corner of Essex. Take minor roads south from the A505, or north from the B1039. The pub is at the centre of the village, almost opposite the church.

Parking: There is a good car park to one side of the pub.

Length of the walk: 3½ miles (short-cut available). Map: OS Landranger 154 Cambridge, Newmarket and surrounding area (inn GR 461396).

A walk that begins by following part of the local Nature Trail and paths across the fields to Holy Trinity church in the nearby parish of Chrishall. This impressive church, with its notable brasses, once stood in the centre of a thriving village – until the Black Death spread to the countryside! The route returns to Elmdon via present-day Chrishall and field paths.

The Walk

From the pub the walk turns right, and follows the road as far as King's Lane, along which it turns right again. Through a small car park an information board gives details of the Nature Trail and a lidded box contains free leaflets describing what can be seen on the trail.

From here the walk continues ahead to a pond, where it turns left and then bears right, following round behind the pond before bearing left, along the edge of a belt of trees. After a short distance, it crosses to the other side of the trees and up to a corner, where it turns right. After following the hedge for about 50 yards, the walk turns left, through a gap in the hedge. (Keep ahead for a short-cut, see sketch map.)

Through the hedge, the walk follows a path down the side of Park Wood. Where the wood ends, it continues ahead across a meadow to a gap in the hedge, through which it turns right. From here it follows the hedge and, through another gap, the path runs along the other side of Park Wood. After crossing the end of several pastures with views to the left, the walk follows the path as it turns left, along the hedge in front of a large house. Just past the house, the walk turns right, through a small wooden gate leading into the churchyard of Holy Trinity church.

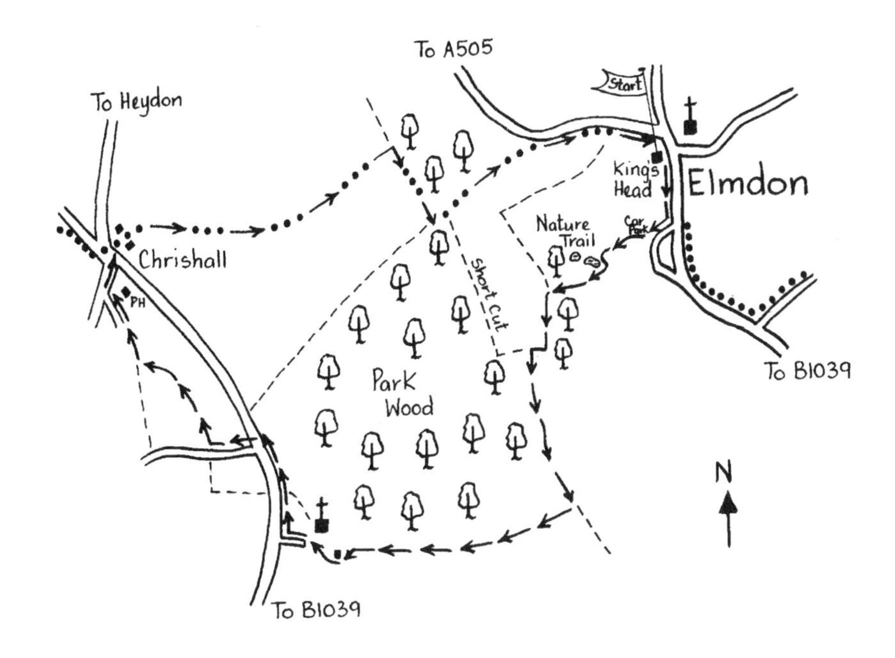

Inside this spacious church there is much to see, including fine brasses, a very large copy of Rubens' masterpiece *The Adoration of the Magi* and an effigy to Lady Margaret de la Pole, dated about 1375. Today, the church appears curiously remote and cut off from its village. Local tradition has it that the first cases of the Black Death in this rural area occurred in Chrishall and that outsiders, desperate to prevent the spread of the plague to their own villages, spared the church, but not the village, which was put to the torch!

From the church the walk follows a path out of the churchyard, past half-timbered cottages and down to a road. Here, it turns right and stays with the road up a rise before turning left, along a very narrow lane. The lane is followed as far as a cast-iron handpump on the verge to the right, where the walk turns right, along a field-edge path. In the corner it turns left, and continues along the edge of the field before turning right, along another path. The path soon becomes a narrow lane leading through the outskirts of Chrishall and, within a short distance, the walk passes the Red Cow public house. Past the pub, the walk turns right, up to a crossroads, across which it joins the Icknield Way Path as it runs through a garage yard.

At the rear of the garage yard the walk continues through a metal swing-gate and follows a path ahead over several fields and stiles to the edge of a wood. Here, it rejoins the Nature Trail as it turns right, along a track just inside the trees. At a cross-tracks it turns left, and follows a track for a short distance to a road. Here, the walk turns right, back to the pub.

Icknield Way Path – Elmdon to Great Chesterford (5 miles)

Along this section of the Icknield Way Path green lanes skirting woods contrast with tracks across upland prairies before the route crosses the M11.

From the King's Head the route follows the road, see above, before turning left, along the farm road to Freewood Farm. At the farm it turns left, on a bridleway, then right, on a green lane which runs for about ½ mile to a cross-tracks over which the track eventually becomes a narrow tarmac lane past a row of cottages. Between cottages the route turns left, down a path which joins another tarmac lane, uphill, past Strethall church. The lane bears right and runs down to a T-junction, where it turns left, along a road. Over a crossroads it turns right, on a field path across prairie-like fields to the far corner where the route follows a hedged path along the line of an old Roman road. Eventually, a footbridge is crossed over the M11, from where a track runs past houses on the outskirts of Great Chesterford. At the railway it turns left, then right, over the line, on a road leading to a main road.

Here, the route turns left, over a branch of the river Cam and up a short hill before turning right, along Church Street. After passing the Crown and Thistle, a public house that offers bed and breakfast accommodation, the route turns right, along Rose Lane. From here the route is described in the next pub walk.

[14] **Great Chesterford** (Essex)
The Plough

Great Chesterford was once a walled Roman town, complete with fort and well served by Roman roads. Today, all signs of the enclosing wall have long since disappeared, and the M11 bypasses a village in which one sign of busier days is the number of ex-pubs that have been converted to houses.

The Plough stands at the eastern end of the High Street which once boasted as many as a dozen pubs! It is a handsome, pink-washed and tiled building, parts of which date back to the 16th century when it housed the village cobbler at one end and a pub at the other. Now, the pub occupies the whole building plus a modern extension to the rear. Exposed ceiling and wall beams, quarry tiles, and open fireplaces combine to create a homely, country atmosphere. Copper and brass gleam in nooks and crannies whilst the new extension provides light and airiness to the bar. Home-cooked food, served in separate dining areas, includes bar meals such as beef and ale pie, with fresh fish a permanent (and also take-away) speciality. Restaurant dishes include steaks, poached salmon in sherry cream sauce, or pork fillet in sage sauce with apricots – all of which can be rounded off with a choice of home-made desserts. A vegetarian selection is always available. Children are welcome in the family/games room or the dining areas and also have their own adventure

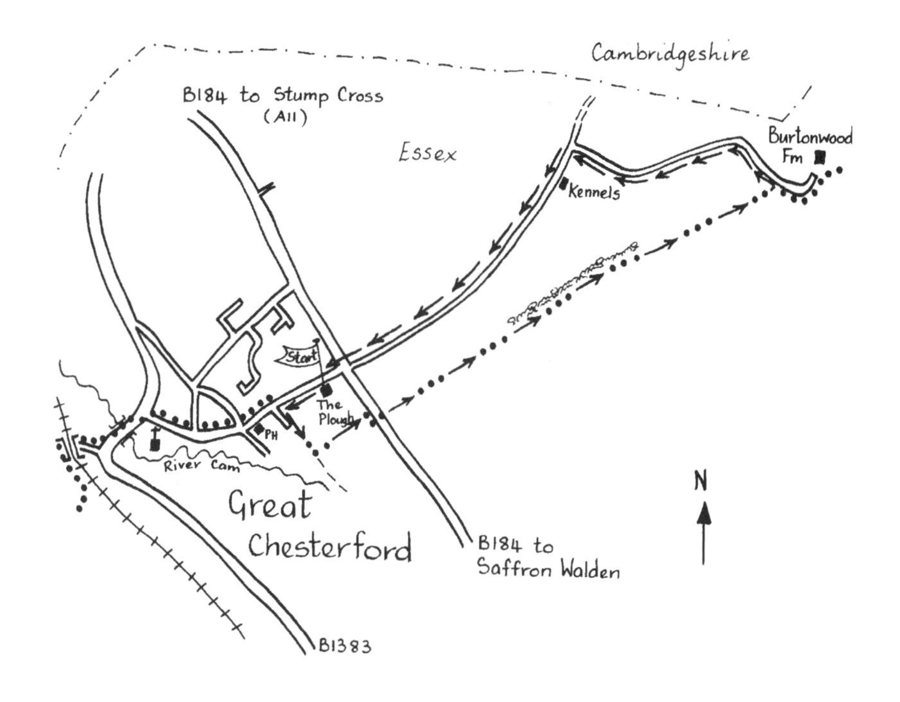

playground at the bottom of the pleasant gardens behind the pub.

The Plough is a Greene King pub and serves their Abbot Ale, IPA, XX Mild and a seasonal bitter. Guinness, Murphy's, cider and lager are also available on draught.

The opening hours are Monday to Saturday from 11 am to 3 pm and 6 pm to 11.30 pm, and on Sunday from noon to 10.30 pm.

Telephone: 01799 530283.

How to get there: Great Chesterford lies to the east of the M11, just inside the Essex border, only 3 miles north-west of Saffron Walden. From Stump Cross (the junction of the A1301 and the A11), follow either the B184 or the B1383 south to the village. Or, from Saffron Walden, follow the B184 north. The pub is on the High Street at the eastern edge of the village.

Parking: There is a good car park to the rear of the pub.

Length of the walk: 3 miles. Map: OS Landranger 154 Cambridge, Newmarket and surrounding area (inn GR 512429).

A delightful circuit with fine views across rolling, farming uplands and easy walking on the return leg.

The Walk

From the pub the walk turns left, along the High Street.

A short distance down the High Street the walk joins the Icknield Way Path as it turns left, along Rose Lane. Past the village hall and a row of flint and thatched cottages the lane ends and the route continues ahead on a path to a T-junction with a gravelled track. Here, the walk turns left, and follows the track up to a road.

At the road it turns right, then left, as it crosses the road to follow a field edge track running up to the top of a long rise. From here there are the first good views of the village below and across the shallow valley to the north. Further on the track keeps to the right of a high hedge across undulating, arable fields. Where the hedge ends the walk leaves the track as it keeps ahead on a footpath across a wide, arable field. On the far side of the field the path goes through the hedge to meet the farm access road to nearby Burtonwood Farm.

Here, the Icknield Way Path turns right, but the pub walk turns left and follows the road downhill. After bending left, the road provides over a mile of pleasant, easy walking as it winds along the bottom of the shallow valley. At a junction with a track the route stays with the road which, along this stretch, is also used by riders on the Icknield Way Riders' Route. Past an isolated kennels and cattery, the road continues to follow the valley before, eventually, meeting a main road. Over the road, the walk follows the High Street back to the pub.

Icknield Way Path – Great Chesterford to Linton (5 miles)

There are good views along this stretch, which crosses rolling, upland farmland.

For the route from Great Chesterford to the access road to Burtonwood Farm, see above. Having turned right on the road leading to the farm, the route turns left, on a track past the farmhouse and barns. Just past the barns on the left, it turns right, along a track which bears left, and then continues in roughly the same direction across upland, arable fields. Eventually, a field-edge track leads down and under the overhead National Grid lines to a corner. From here it follows a narrow, hedged path which emerges at the top of a wide, downhill farm track. Here, the route turns right, along the track, down to a road along which it turns left, into Cambridgeshire.

Past Linton Zoo, just before the A604, the route turns left, along The Grip, up to the Green Hill public house. Here it crosses the A604 and runs down the High Street, past the Crown Inn (bed and breakfast). At the bottom of the hill, just before the bridge over the river Granta, it turns left, along Meadow Lane. From here the route is described in the next pub walk.

[15] **Linton** (Cambridgeshire)
The Dog and Duck

Linton has many attractions, including a zoo and nearby Chilford Hall, Cambridgeshire's largest vineyard.

The thatched Dog and Duck stands next to the bridge over the river Granta at the bottom of the High Street in the centre of the village. Converted to its present use over 100 years ago, the pub's name apparently derives from the ancient 'sport' of duck baiting, about which, perhaps, the less said the better – ask the landlord! Inside, heavily beamed ceilings and open fireplaces are complemented by brasses and pictures, including old photographs of the pub. A long bar serves an open-plan area, one end of which is used for dining. A good range of very reasonably priced bar meals includes traditional pub grub, such as cottage pies and steak and kidney pies, plus a selection of steaks. Sunday lunch is prepared from fresh, local produce, with choice meat from the butcher's just along the High Street. Vegetarians are catered for and children's portions are available. Dogs on a lead are allowed in the non-dining area of the bar, whilst behind the pub is a riverside garden.

The Dog and Duck is a Greene King pub and serves their IPA, Abbot Ale and XX Mild, plus a seasonal ale. Brewers Bitter, Guinness, Murphy's, cider and lager are also available on draught.

The opening times are Monday to Saturday from 11.30 am to 3 pm and 5.30 pm to 11 pm, and on Sunday from noon to 10.30 pm.
Telephone: 01223 891257.

How to get there: Linton is in the south-east corner of Cambridgeshire, near the Essex border. The village is on the northern side of the A604 (Cambridge to Haverhill) just 2 miles east of the A11(T). Turn off the A604 to follow the High Street down to the pub.

Parking: There is a good car park to the rear of the pub.

Length of the walk: 2½ miles (extensions available). Map: OS Landranger 154 Cambridge, Newmarket and surrounding area (inn GR 561468).

A short walk up to the water tower on the top of Rivey Hill, with good views of Linton in the valley below. Down the hill again, the walk follows back streets and the river Granta through this picturesque village. Possible extensions include Chilford Hall Vineyard to the north, or Linton Zoo to the south (see sketch map).

The Walk

From the pub the walk joins the Icknield Way Path as it turns right, along Meadow Lane. Where the lane ends it keeps ahead on a tarmac path down one side of a riverside recreation ground. At the far end it turns right, past the cricket pavilion and over a footbridge across the river Granta. From here the walk follows a path which leads ahead to a back road, over which it continues through a bungalow estate and along a service road, up to a main road.

At the road the walk turns right for a few yards then crosses the road as it turns left, along a bridleway signposted to Rivey Hill. The walk stays with the track as it runs uphill, across arable fields, before keeping to the right of a wood. At the top it turns right, along the ridge.

From this high ground there are wide views across the valley below and westwards, to Hadstock and beyond. Aircraft hangars silhouetted on the distant skyline were used by Mustangs of the United States 8th Army Air Force, USAAF, based at Little Walden during the Second World War. In addition to the hangars, the conning tower and some stretches of perimeter track survive as a reminder of less peaceful days when virtually the whole of East Anglia was one vast military base and airfield.

The walk follows the track, which keeps to the left of another wood before passing a converted barn and a flint-faced cottage opposite the red-brick water tower. Built in 1936, the 92 ft tower supplied Linton with its first mains water and makes a prominent landmark, visible for miles across the surrounding countryside.

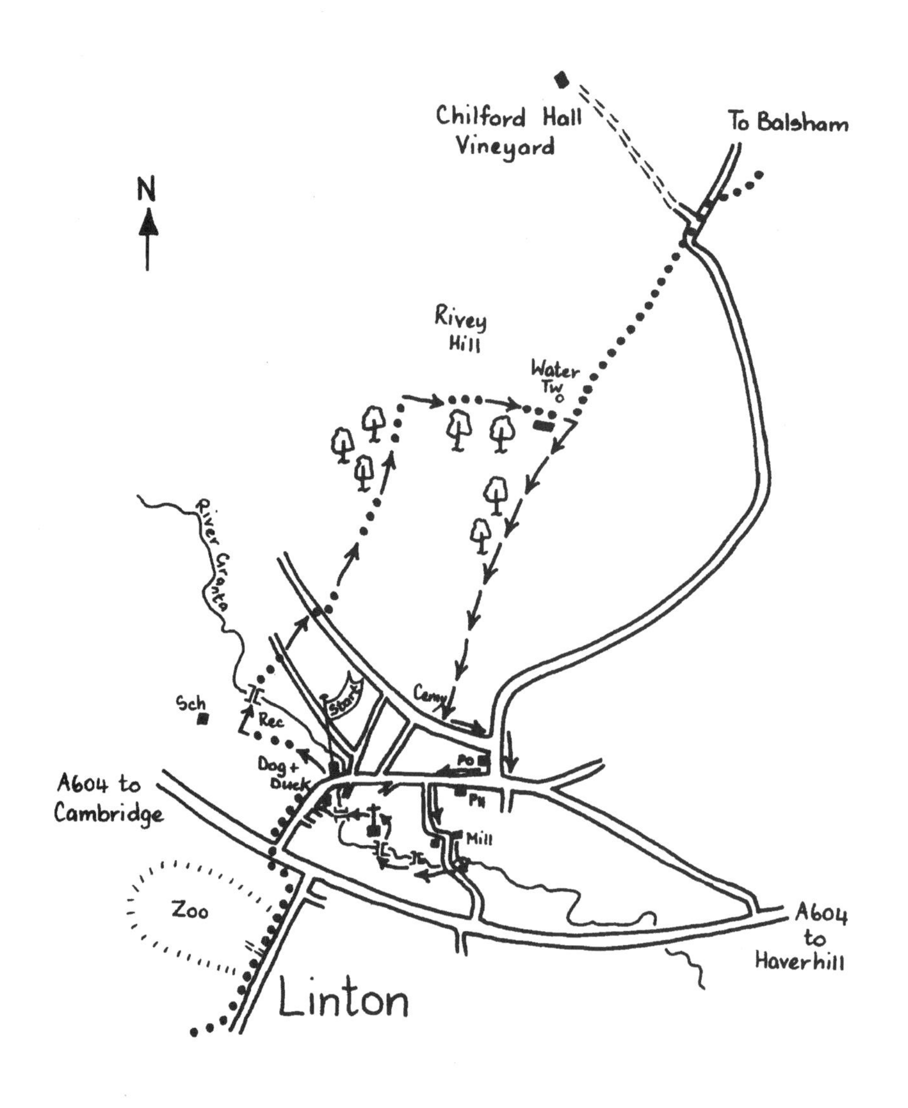

Here, the walk can be extended by staying with the Icknield Way Path, which turns left, down to a road, a few yards along which is the entrance to Chilford Hall Vineyard, open to visitors from Easter to the end of September, telephone: 01223 892641.

The pub walk, however, turns right and runs downhill, on a sunken track along the edge of the wood. The track gets muddier as it runs down to the spring-line, below which the banks on either side provide easier going. At the bottom of the hill the track continues ahead through council houses and past a cemetery to a road. Here, it turns left to a junction, where it turns right, past the village post office which sells a comprehensive guide to the village and its history. At the T-junction just past the post office, the walk turns right again, along the High Street. Past the Waggon and Horses public house it turns left, down Mill Lane. At the mill it turns right, between the buildings, and follows the lane down to a ford and footbridge over the river Granta. Across the river the walk turns right, along a river-bank footpath. Past a first footbridge, it eventually turns right, over another footbridge, to follow a tarmac path through the churchyard of St Mary's. Just past the church itself it turns left, at cross paths, and exits the churchyard opposite an impressive 16th-century, pargeted building, known as the Guildhall.

From here the walk crosses over the lane leading to the church and runs down the left-hand side of the Guildhall, past which it arrives at a last footbridge across the river. Over this it follows a narrow lane leading back to the High Street, where it turns right, back down to the pub.

Icknield Way Path – Linton to Brinkley (10 miles)

Vineyards and Roman roads make this a varied section with the milestone at Balsham recording completion of over half the distance along the Icknield Way Path.

For the route from Linton to the water tower on Rivey Hill, see above. From the tower the route turns left, down to the road, which is followed past the entrance to Chilford Hall Vineyard (see above). Shortly, it turns off the road on a footpath to the right which crosses several arable fields before turning right on a wide track (Roman road). At a T-junction it turns left, up and over a rise, beyond which the track becomes Wood Hall Lane leading to Balsham.

Crossing over a road, the route keeps to the right-hand side of the triangular village green, where the opening ceremony was held when the Icknield Way Path was designated a Regional Recreational Route in September 1992.

Past the church and through a small car park, the route turns left, along a field-edge path. After crossing several stiles, it turns right and follows a wide track for about a mile. After crossing a road and a narrow lane, the track eventually turns right, in front of a pumping station, after which it meets another lane. Here it turns left, and follows the lane over a rise before turning right, along another track, across open farmland leading to Cricks Farm. Past farm buildings, the track bends right at a pond, but the route follows a path ahead, up and over an arable field. On the far side it keeps to the left of a wire fence to another road. Here, it turns right to the T-junction, where it turns left, through a swing-gate. From here the route follows a path across paddocks before joining a track leading into Brinkley. From here the route is described in the next pub walk.

[16] **Brinkley** (Cambridgeshire)

The Red Lion

Brinkley lies on high ground and basks in rural tranquillity, as peaceful a staging post as any to be found along the route of the Icknield Way Path.

The Red Lion, originally a farmhouse, was converted to its present use in 1709. In addition to bed and breakfast accommodation, there are two separate bars, a public bar with pool table and games, and a lounge bar which extends to a small restaurant at one end. The ceilings are heavily beamed and low in places – be warned! The home-cooked bar meals include favourites such as steak and kidney pies, or daily 'specials', such as liver and bacon. Tables with cheerful gingham table-cloths and wheelback chairs furnish the attractive restaurant, in which the menu offers more exotic dishes, for example duck or guinea fowl in orange or black cherry sauce, in addition to which there is a choice of three roasts on a Sunday. Children's portions are available and there is also a vegetarian option. Meals are not served on Mondays, when the restaurant is closed. Dogs kept on a lead are allowed in the bar, but not in the restaurant. A large garden complete with petanque is to be found to the front and one side of the pub, plus a small paddock and resident horse to the rear.

The Red Lion is a Greene King pub and serves their Abbot Ale and IPA. Guinness and draught lager are also available.

The opening times are Monday to Saturday from 11 am to 3 pm and 6 pm to 11 pm, and on Sunday from noon to 10.30 pm.
Telephone: 01638 508285.

How to get there: Brinkley is on the B1052, 5 miles south of Newmarket. Take the B1061 due south from Newmarket, or follow minor roads off the A1304 around Six Mile Bottom. The pub is on the west of the village on the Six Mile Bottom road.

Parking: There is a car park in front of the pub.

Length of the walk: 2½ miles (longer extension available). Map: OS Landranger 154 Cambridge, Newmarket and surrounding area (inn GR 626548).

An easy, pleasant stroll to nearby Burrough Green with its ancient church and one of the best examples of a village green in Cambridgeshire. The return is via field paths along which the walk can be extended (see sketch map), to include a visit to the parish church of Westley Waterless, notable for its 14th-century brasses.

The Walk

From the pub the walk turns right, along the road. At the next two junctions it keeps ahead on the roadside path. Opposite the village post office stands St Mary's church, inside which the ensign of HMS *Brinkley* hangs over the box-pews as unexpected evidence of the long association between this rural, inland village and the Senior Service.

Past the church the walk joins the Icknield Way Path, which comes in on a track to the right. The walk stays with the road as far as the red telephone box, where it turns left, on a footpath signposted to Burrough Green. The fenced path continues ahead before crossing a substantial footbridge with a stile at each end. From here the walk follows a path alongside a wooden railed fence down the side of a paddock. Over a stile and footbridge in the corner, it keeps to the field edge before bearing right, across the crop, then left, over another footbridge, to a high, three-step stile into another paddock. Here, it turns right to the corner, then left, as it follows round the field to another three-step stile on the right. Over this and a footbridge, it turns left, along a service road leading to Burrough Green.

Past a small pond on the right, the walk emerges on the edge of a wide village green. From here the Icknield Way Path crosses the green and continues down the right-hand side of the Bull public house. The pub walk, however, turns left, along a narrow lane leading to the parish church. Just before the lane ends, the walk turns right, on a path through the churchyard. Past the main entrance porch to the ancient church it leaves via a swing-gate in the corner. From here it follows a track which keeps ahead, through

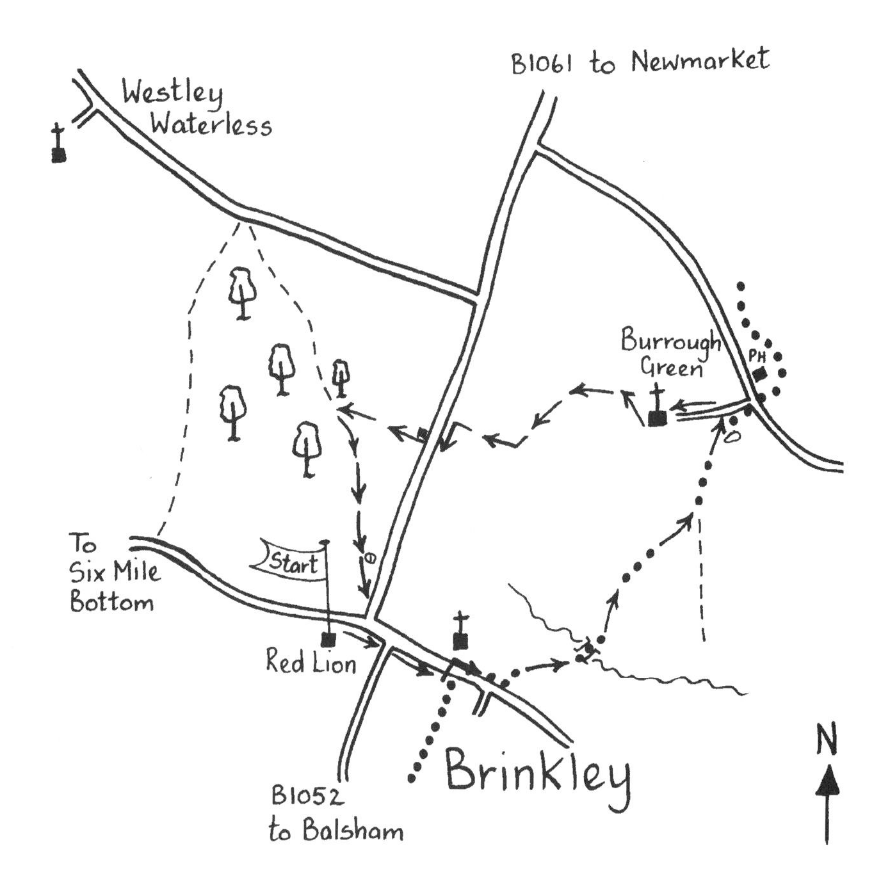

another gate and over a drive serving a farmyard on the right, Eventually, the path becomes fenced in, squeezed between paddocks, on the other side of which it turns left. In the next corner it turns right, through the hedge, to turn right on a grassy track leading to a road.

At the road it turns left, for a short distance, then right, on a footpath leading down the left-hand side of a house. From here it keeps ahead across wide, flat, arable fields before turning left at a T-junction. (Turn right for the extension to the church at Westley Waterless – see sketch map.)

Having turned left, the main walk follows a path to the right of a ditch across arable fields with good views across open farmland to the right. Eventually, at a pond on the left, the walk follows a path that bears right, cutting across the corner of the field to the nearby road. Crossing over the road to the roadside path, the walk turns right, up to the T-junction, where it turns right again, back to the pub.

Icknield Way Path – Brinkley to past Stetchworth (3 miles)

A 'horsey' stretch as the route approaches Newmarket, the capital of horse-racing.

For the route from Brinkley to Burrough Green, see above. Having followed the track down the right-hand side of the Bull public house, the route turns left, on a path behind the pub and a row of houses. Across an open field, it aims to the left of the row of cottages on the far side, where it turns right, on a track for about ½ mile. At a road it crosses straight over to follow a path to the left of paddock rails. Over a ditch, it turns right, for a few yards, then left, on a path sandwiched between paddocks. The path runs ahead, over a drive, and squeezes through a gap at the end, turning left, along the edge of a wood (now in company with the Stour Valley Path, which runs for 60 miles, from Newmarket to Cattawade on the Suffolk coast).

At the corner of the wood the route turns right, across a ditch, to follow the trees for a few yards before turning left, along a ditch running down the side of a wide field. At a corner it dog-legs left, then right, down and out of a sunken track before running ahead over stiles across more paddocks. Over a stile and cross-tracks, the route keeps ahead to a road, along which it turns left into Stetchworth. Opposite the Marquis of Granby public house, it turns right, on a footpath through houses and across a service road. Clear of the houses, a field-edge track is followed down and over a cross-tracks. From here the route is described in the next pub walk.

[17] **Woodditton** (Cambridgeshire)
The Three Blackbirds

Situated on the eastern edge of Cambridgeshire, Woodditton lies at the southern end of the Devil's Dyke, one of five long dykes along the Icknield Way.

The Three Blackbirds has a long tradition of hospitality, as shown by the date 1642 on its white walls. Inside, the pub offers very comfortable, five-star accommodation, with two separate bars, a restaurant area and an upstairs lounge. Exposed beams and brickwork complemented by open fireplaces combine to create everyone's idea of the ideal country pub, steeped in tradition and comfort. All the meals are home-made, from bar food, such as beef in Guinness pie, to a wide choice of à la carte dishes, including seafood thermidor, or venison casserole. A tempting range of desserts includes summer pudding, an all-year-round favourite. There is always a choice for vegetarians and the upstairs smoking/coffee lounge allows for a no-smoking rule in the restaurant. During the week walkers are allowed to bring their own sandwiches, providing that they buy a drink – a policy that has made this pub a mecca for local ramblers! Groups must phone to confirm this arrangement in advance. Dogs are not allowed inside, but there are very pleasant gardens to the front and side of the pub.

This is a Pubmaster pub and it serves Greene King IPA, Tetley Bitter and

Ansells Bitter. Guinness, cider and lager are also available on draught.

The opening times are Monday to Saturday from 11.30 am to 2.30 pm and 6.30 pm to 11 pm, and on Sunday from noon to 10.30 pm.

Telephone: 01638 730811.

How to get there: Woodditton is 3 miles south of Newmarket. Take the B1061 due south and turn off east, to follow minor roads. The pub is at the centre of the village, opposite a magnificent horse-chestnut tree.

Parking: There is a car park to the rear of the pub.

Length of the walk: 3 miles (short-cut available). Map: OS Landranger 154 Cambridge, Newmarket and surrounding area (inn GR 660582).

An easy but interesting walk which follows a section of the Devil's Dyke through woodland, then field paths across pleasant, open countryside.

The Walk

From the pub the walk turns right. The road is followed as it bends right, then left, past the water tower, a prominent, local landmark. Ignoring the track on the bend, it continues along the road for a short distance before turning right, on a footpath signposted to Newmarket and Reach.

The walk stays with the path, which runs ahead across an arable field, on the other side of which it enters Pickmore Wood and bears right, not far from the line of the huge ditch known as Devil's Dyke, the largest earthwork of its type in the country. Consisting of a ditch and rampart, 30 metres wide and up to 18 metres high, it is believed to have been excavated as a defensive barrier along tribal boundaries around the 6th century AD. Whatever its original purpose, it was a stupendous undertaking for its time and has, as its name indicates, remained something of a superstitious wonder over the centuries. Today, it has been designated a Site of Special Scientific Interest (SSSI), as its length provides a refuge for wildlife and some of the few surviving areas of chalk grasslands in this region of intensive farming.

After a while, the woodland path bears left and emerges in the corner of a large field. Here, a short-cut can be taken by turning right (see sketch map). The main walk, however, turns left, along a path and hedge up rising ground to a broad track, where it turns right and, eventually, runs down to a cross-tracks.

Here, just below the nearby village of Stetchworth, the walk joins the Icknield Way Path as it turns right. Along this short, downhill stretch, it also joins the Stour Valley Path, which runs for 60 miles from Newmarket to Cattawade on the Suffolk coast. At the bottom of the hill the walk is rejoined by the short-cut, which comes in from the right. The Stour Valley Path turns off left, along the line of the Devil's Dyke, but the main walk stays with the

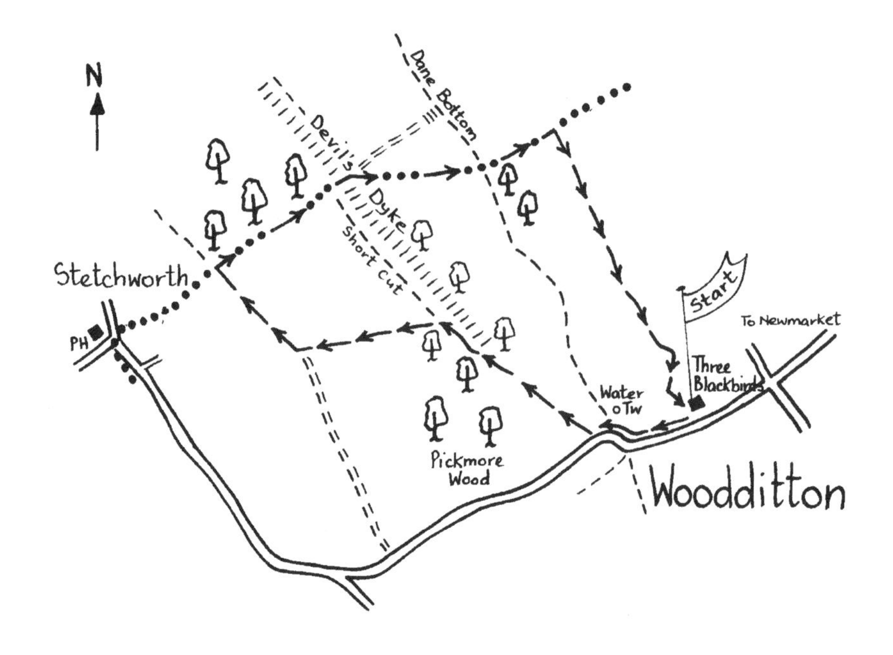

Icknield Way Path which keeps ahead, across the dyke. On the other side of the dyke it ignores the track ahead and bears right, on a field path leading over the crest of a wide, arable field with good views to the north. On the other side of the field the path runs down to a T-junction on a track known as Dane Bottom. Here, the walk crosses over and follows the uphill track ahead. Almost at the top of the rise the walk leaves the Icknield Way Path, which continues ahead, as it turns right, on a path to the left of a hedge.

At the corner of the field the route keeps ahead, through a gap in the hedge. From here the walk continues on a path that bears right, across an arable field, aiming for the oak tree to the left of the distant water tower. Over a stile it keeps to the left-hand side of a field, almost to the bottom corner, where it turns left, opposite the tower. Over a footbridge it turns right and, within a short distance, emerges at the car park to the rear of the pub.

Icknield Way Path – past Dane Bottom to Ashley (4½ miles)

For the route from Stetchworth to the top of the rise past Dane Bottom, see above.

The next stretch starts with good tracks across open, arable farmland before crossing more 'horse' country.

A thatcher at work along the route.

From the top of the rise the route continues ahead to a road, along which it turns right, then goes left, down Maypole Lane. Past the church, where the lane bends right, it keeps ahead along a farm access road which eventually becomes a track. This runs for about ½ mile across wide, arable fields before bending left, at which point a path is followed ahead, through a small wood, and across a field to a road. Over the road, it follows a fenced bridleway for about a mile before emerging on the road into Cheveley, along which it turns left. From here the route is described in the next pub walk.

[18] **Ashley** (Cambridgeshire)
The Crown

Ashley is close to Newmarket, historic centre of English racing, home to the Jockey Club, the National Stud and the National Horse-racing Museum. In Newmarket, as befits a 'capital' where the horse is king, everything stops for horses – literally – and the surrounding, park-like countryside is studded with luxurious stables.

Situated on the Newmarket road in the centre of the village, the Crown is an unpretentious 'local'. Built as a coaching inn over 250 years ago, its open-plan bar room provides space for a dining area at one end, and games at the other. A gesture is made to the 'sport of kings' in that prints and photographs of horses adorn the walls, but the sporting trophies on display range from darts to petanque. An open fireplace at one end, a log-burner at the other, plus easy-going, friendly management, ensures a warm reception at any time of the year. A range of value-for-money, home-cooked pub grub includes queen and king-sized servings of all the usual favourites, from shepherd's pie to fisherman's bake, plus a daily 'special' and traditional roast dinner on a Sunday. Vegetarians can be catered for with prior notice, and children's portions of everything are served. Meals are not available at lunchtimes on Wednesday, when the pub is shut. There is a children's play area in the garden behind the pub where a barbecue operates at weekends during the summer. Dogs on a lead are allowed inside, but not in the dining area.

The Crown is a Greene King pub and serves their IPA, Abbot Ale and seasonal bitter. Guinness, lager and cider are also available on draught.

The opening times are Monday to Saturday from noon to 3 pm and 5.30 pm to 11 pm (closed Wednesday lunchtime), and on Sunday from noon to 10.30 pm.

Telephone: 01638 730737.

How to get there: Ashley is 3 miles south-east of Newmarket, just on the Cambridgeshire side of the border with Suffolk. Take the B1063 from Newmarket, which runs through the village, with the pub at its centre.

Parking: There is a car park in front of the pub.

Length of the walk: 3½ miles. Map: OS Landranger 154 Cambridge, Newmarket and surrounding area (inn GR 697616).

A pleasant, undemanding walk that provides tantalising glimpses of a world in which stud farms decorate park-like countryside, tailor-made regardless of expense to suit the pampered requirements of even the most discerning of blue-blooded horses!

The Walk

The walk crosses over to follow the B1063 opposite the pub. Past the post office and the Old Plough, now a licensed restaurant, the roadside path ends just short of the top of the hill. From here care must be taken as the road is followed over the top of the hill and down to a footpath on the right.

Having turned right, the walk follows the path, which runs downhill diagonally to the right, across a wide field of cereal crops. There are good views across open countryside to the south-east and, at the far corner, the path bears left, along the edge of a small wood to a lane. Here the walk turns right, on the closely cut roadside verge which provides easy walking past the grand entrance to a succession of stud farms and not-so-mini mansions. Eventually, it reaches Broad Green, which is faced by some very attractive houses. Here, the walk crosses diagonally right, over to the corner of the green to a track signposted to Cheveley. From here it keeps ahead as the track becomes a hedged path between paddocks awash with brood mares and foals. Appropriately enough, this path ends at a large stables complex where the walk turns right, then left, along a service road or drive, which leads out of the stables to the road into Cheveley.

The walk now joins the Icknield Way Path as it turns right, and follows the road through the village. Within a short distance, St Mary's church is passed on the right, a 13th-century, flint-faced building, unusual

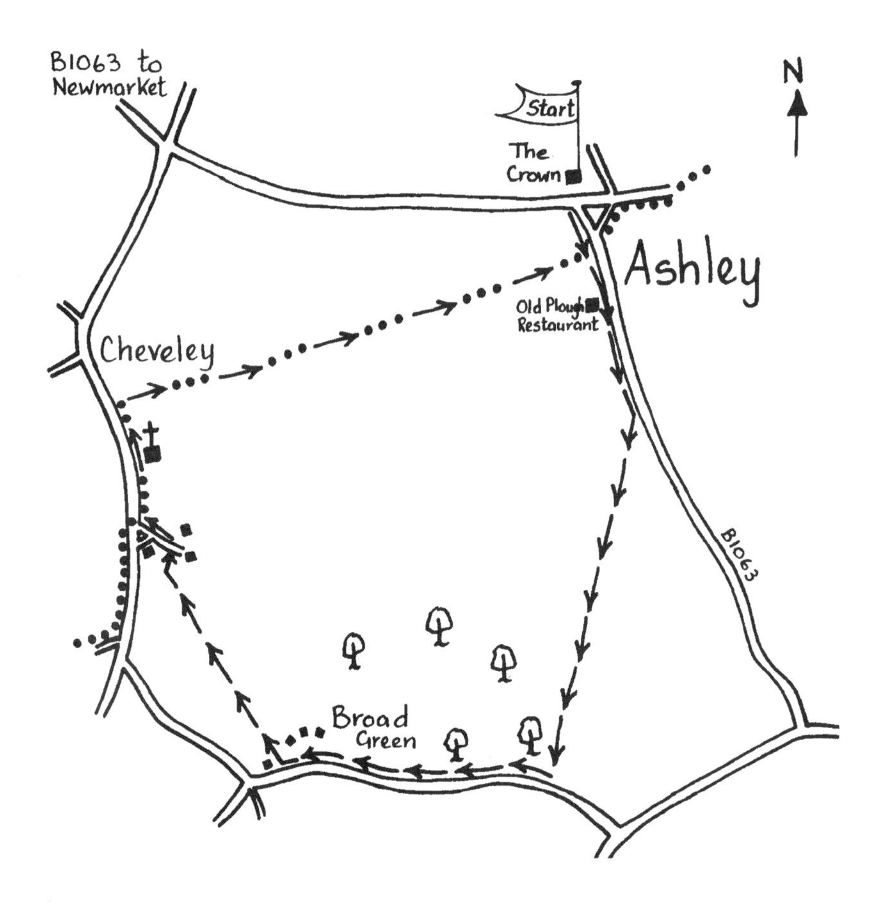

for its tower staircase added to one corner and its external bells. There are some interesting houses clustered round the church, including one dated 1756 with original, lead-glazed windows.

Further down the High Street, the walk turns right, on a waymarked path to the left of number 119. From here it follows another hedged path as it runs ahead with more paddocks and horse gallops to the left and meadows to the right. Over a drive to another stud farm, the path continues ahead across more open farmland for about a mile before bearing left, along the hedge, as more paddocks close in on the right. Eventually, the path emerges on the road to the left of the Old Plough ex-pub, where the walk turns left, back down to the Crown.

Icknield Way Path – Ashley to the river Kennett (1 mile)

For the route from Cheveley to Ashley, see above.

This short stretch follows quiet, minor roads as the route crosses into

The packhorse bridge at Moulton, Suffolk.

Suffolk. From Ashley the route turns right, past the village pond, on the road to Gazeley. At a fork in the road it bears left, and follows the road downhill, across the B1085, and into Suffolk. The road continues ahead and the route eventually turns off to the right, just before Catford Bridge over the river Kennett. From here the route is described in the next pub walk.

[19] **Moulton** (Suffolk)
The King's Head

Moulton lies on what was the Cambridge to Bury St Edmunds packhorse route and a 15th century packhorse bridge still stands across the river Kennett, not far from the King's Head.

The pub is a rambling, Victorian, yellow-brick building, spacious enough to accommodate two separate bars and a very pleasant dining room. In addition to the usual furnishings, the lounge displays locally crafted walking sticks and hand-made pottery. Chalkboard menus may offer a range of griddled steaks, barbecued ribs, fresh trout or locally made sausages. Bar meals include 'mega' toasted sandwiches with a wide choice of fillings. Vegetarians and children have their own daily selection. Dogs are not allowed inside, but there are two gardens. One, by the dining room, has been designated a 'child free zone', and the other, to the rear, is a family garden, complete with play facilities for children.

The King's Head is a Greene King pub and serves their IPA and Abbot Ale plus a seasonal choice. Guinness, cider and lager are also available on draught.

The pub is closed all day on a Monday. Opening times for the rest of the week are Tuesday to Saturday from noon to 3 pm and 6.30 pm to 11 pm, and on Sunday from noon to 10.30 pm.

Telephone: 01638 750156.

How to get there: Moulton is just over 2 miles east of Newmarket, between the B1506 and the B1063, on the B1085 Kentford to Dalham road. The pub is on the eastern side of the village near the river Kennett.

Parking: There is a car park behind the pub.

Length of the walk: 6½ miles (short-cuts available). Map: OS Landranger 154 Cambridge, Newmarket and surrounding area (inn GR 697645).

An interesting and varied walk that follows the Three Churches way-marked, circular route established by Suffolk County Council. The walk links the three churches and villages of Moulton, Dalham and Gazeley and includes over 3 miles of the Icknield Way Path.

The Walk

From the pub the walk turns left, down to the ancient packhorse bridge maintained by English Heritage. Just before the bridge is reached it turns right, on a path along the bank of the river Kennett. Past two bridges followed by a modern ford, it turns left, across a road bridge over the river. On the other side it turns right, along the roadside verge and past the gates to St Peter's church on the opposite side of the road.

Where the road ends, the walk continues ahead on the left-hand bank of the river, which meanders away from time to time. Further on, the path keeps to the left of a high hedge as it crosses arable fields, after which a tree-lined track stays with the river almost to the road. At the road a first short-cut can be taken by turning left (see sketch map). However, the main walk turns right, and follows the road over Catford Bridge across the river.

Over the bridge, the walk joins the Icknield Way Path as it turns left, through the trees, to the right-hand bank of the river. From here it follows the willow-lined riverbank for almost a mile before crossing a stile, beyond which it turns left, over a footbridge across the river. Here, the walk turns left again, along a road through the picturesque village of Dalham. Past the ancient, conical Malt Kiln and the road to the church, the walk turns right, on a footpath leading between an avenue of mature chestnut trees. (Stay with the road for another short-cut – see sketch map.)

The path leads up to St Mary's church, to the right of Dalham Hall, once owned by Cecil Rhodes, the South African statesman. Through a swing-gate the walk turns right, along a narrow lane, past the front of the church. At a Y-junction it forks left, up to the top of a rise. Here, the walk turns left, on a path running through woods. Out of the trees, it keeps ahead, with the woodland now on the left, and follows a path down, then up to a corner, where it turns left, back into the woods again. The path bears right and keeps just inside the edge of some more mature trees for a good

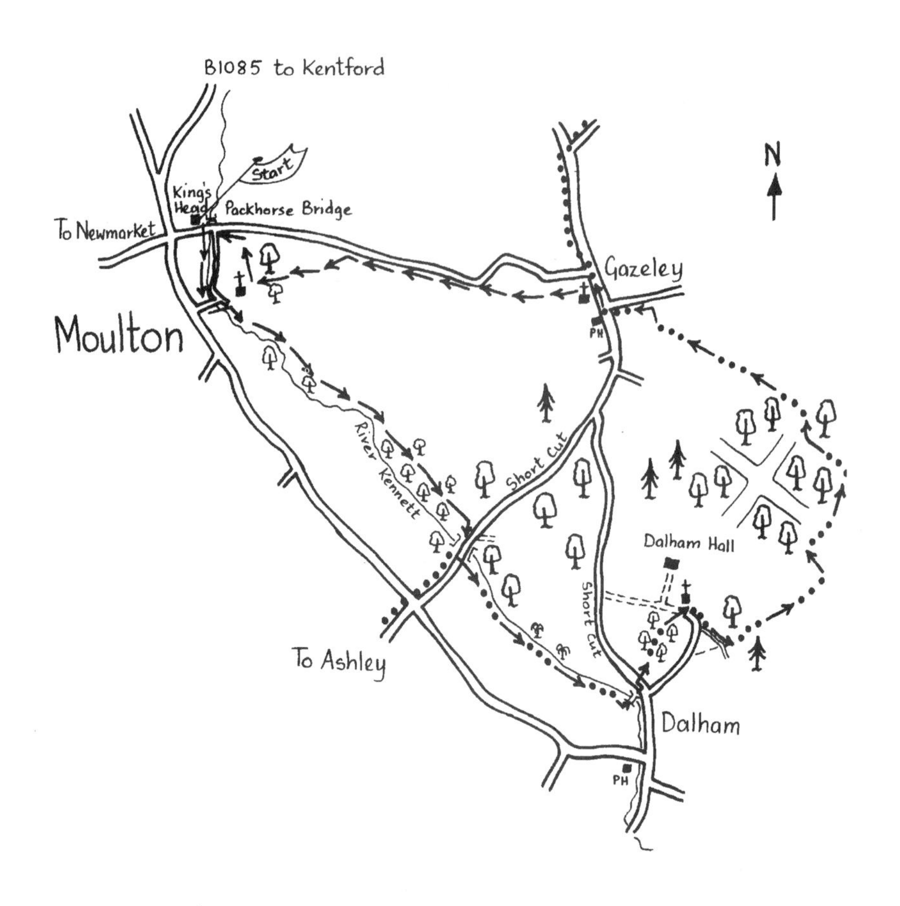

distance. Out of the woods again, the walk keeps ahead to a corner, where it runs back into the trees, staying with the path as it winds through them. After bearing left, it turns right, along the edge of the woodland to a corner, from which the path follows a wire fence through more trees.

Eventually, clear of the woods for the last time, the walk turns left, over a footbridge, and keeps ahead on field-edge paths, with Gazeley church in sight across open fields ahead. The path continues between two arable fields and across a narrow field to a stile, from which a walled path runs between houses on the outskirts of Gazeley. Over a service road, it follows a tarmac path which bears left to a road, along which the walk turns left.

At a T-junction opposite the Chequers public house, the short-cut routes rejoin the main walk as it turns right. The Icknield Way Path stays with the road but, just past All Saints' church, the pub walk turns left, on a footpath across the end of the churchyard. Behind the church, it follows a hedged path past stables and paddocks before, eventually, joining a minor road at a bend. Here, the walk keeps ahead, and follows the road for about ¼ mile. As the road starts to run downhill, the route turns left, on a footpath across arable fields. The path crosses a wide field with good views across open farmland before running downhill to a stile. From here it continues down, through trees and emerges at the rear of St Peter's church.

Here, the walk turns right, on a narrow path leading to a concrete drive and service road, along which it bears left. At the road junction the walk turns left, and follows the road back down to the packhorse bridge, on the other side of which is the pub.

Icknield Way Path – river Kennett (Catford Bridge) to Icklingham (11 miles)

For the route from Catford Bridge to Gazeley, see above.

The next stretch crosses into the Breckland, an area characterized by a relatively hot, dry climate, open heathland and forests.

Past Gazeley church, the route follows the Kentford road to the top of the hill, where it forks right, on a lane running downhill to cottages at Needham Street. Here, it turns left, down the side of a small green, and across arable fields to the far right-hand corner of a wood. From here a field-edge path leads to the B1506, along which the route turns right. At a fork it turns left, under the main A14 (T) (A45) and a railway bridge, then left again, along a narrow lane. Past silos and gravel pits, the lane becomes a byway track which continues ahead over open heathland for nearly 2 miles before turning right, along a road through Herringswell.

As the road ends, the route continues ahead on a farm road to Hall Farm, past which it dog-legs ahead on a sandy track. Past a belt of mature beech trees, it turns left, over a stile in the corner of a field. From here the route follows a grassy track leading to the road in Tuddenham.

Over the road, it keeps ahead down the side of the village green with its memorial to 90 Squadron, ex RAF Tuddenham. The narrow road becomes a fenced, sandy track which runs for over a mile across Cavenham Heath and its National Nature Reserve. Eventually, a prominent stile on the right marks where a footpath gives the only public access to the open heathland. From here the route is described in the next pub walk.

[20] **Icklingham** (Suffolk)
The Plough Inn

Icklingham is in Breckland, an area straddling the western borders of Suffolk/Norfolk and characterized by a dry climate, open, sandy heathlands and forests. Archaeological finds in this area testify to its settlement long before the medieval, flint and thatched church opposite the pub was built.

The Plough Inn, originally a short terrace of red-brick cottages, was converted to its present use about 200 years ago. Today, its unpretentious exterior conceals comfortable and surprisingly spacious accommodation, made possible by the building of extensions to the rear. From the car park behind the pub the entrance gives access to an L-shaped bar and a main bar room with terracotta tiled floor and open fireplace. The walls display Second World War posters and memorabilia, including a map of the D-Day landings. A games room adjoins this bar, whilst a very pleasant dining room opens off the small area decorated with cricketing prints in front of the bar. Good quality home-cooking ranges from simple bar meals to traditional favourites such as steak and kidney pies, or moussaka for the more adventurous. There is a vegetarian choice and a separate menu for children. Dogs are not allowed inside, but there is a large, attractive garden to the rear, complete with a children's play area.

The Plough Inn is a freehouse and has a good selection of cask ales, including Tetley Bitter, Worthington Best Bitter, Adnams Bitter, Adnams Mild, Greene King IPA, Draught Bass and Boddingtons Bitter. Guinness and lager are also available on draught.

The opening times are Monday to Saturday from 11.30 am to 2.30 pm and 6.30 pm to 11 pm, and on Sunday from noon to 10.30 pm.

Telephone: 01638 711770.

How to get there: Icklingham is on the A1101 (Mildenhall to Bury St Edmunds road), between the A11 and A134, about 6 miles south-west of Thetford. The inn is at the southern end of the village on the main A1101, almost opposite the thatched church.

Parking: There is a fairly large car park to the rear of the pub.

Length of the walk: 4½ miles. Map: OS Landranger 144, Thetford, Breckland and surrounding area (inn GR 775725).

A walk from Icklingham village, with its thatched, medieval church, to Cavenham Heath, one of English Nature's National Nature Reserves. Here a nature 'Discovery Trail', complete with free information leaflet, follows footpaths across sandy, open heathland, characteristic of Breckland.

The Walk

From the pub the walk turns left, along the road through the village. Past the Red Lion and St James' church, it turns left, down West Street. Clear of the houses, it follows a fenced track across flat, open country for some distance before running down to the river Lark, which was once navigable by barges from the Great Ouse north of Ely to Bury St Edmunds. Today, the course of the river is followed from time to time by the Lark Valley Path, which runs for 13 miles between Mildenhall and Bury St Edmunds. Over Temple Bridge, the walk leaves the track as it turns left, through a small car park.

On the other side of the car park is an information board giving details of the nature reserve and from here the walk follows the Discovery Trail. As it crosses the heath the path keeps well to the right of a first concrete pill-box, once part of an outer ring of defences designed to protect wartime RAF Tuddenham.

One of the many bomber bases built throughout East Anglia, RAF Tuddenham opened in 1943 as home to 90 Squadron. Flying Stirlings and Lancasters, the squadron distinguished itself in a wide range of operations, including SOE (Special Operations Executive) missions in support of underground resistance in enemy occupied Europe. Today, nothing is left to mark the site except the old pill-boxes. The runways have long since been broken up for hard-core, and the only operations that noisily continue to the south of here are those connected with the extraction of gravel.

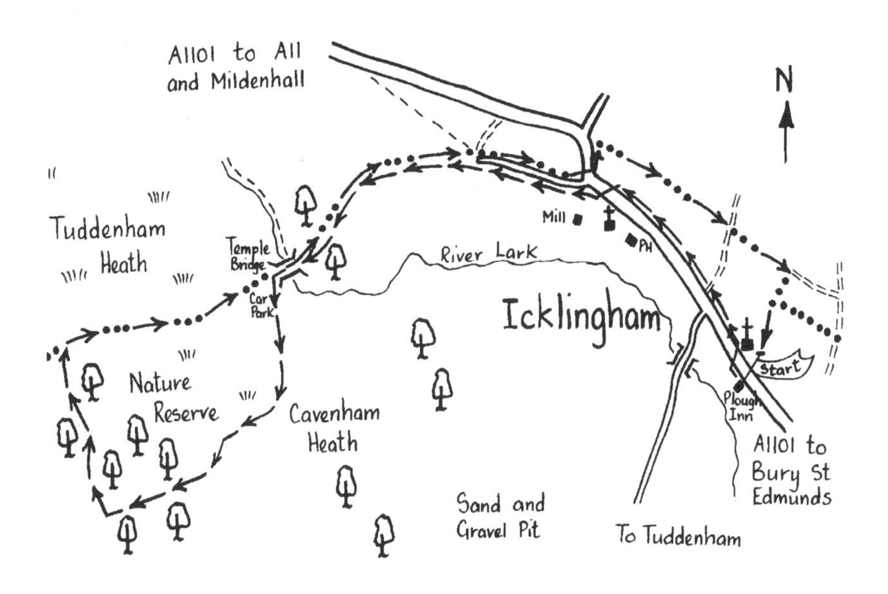

The next stile is designated point No 1 on the eight point Discovery Trail. Here, a green metal box contains free information leaflets, provided by English Nature, giving details of the natural history and wildlife on the heath. Red-topped wooden posts mark the line of the path across the open heath with numbers at intervals relating to the information leaflet. Eventually, the path bears right, through silver-birch woodland. Past a curiously shaped wooden seat, one of a number of wooden 'sculptures', the path turns right and leads up to a last stile next to a broad, sandy track.

Over the stile, the walk joins the Icknield Way Path as it turns right, along the track which was once part of the main route from Norwich to London. After ½ mile or so the track runs down and past the car park where the walk turned off earlier. Back over the river Lark, the outward route is retraced as far as the main road at the top of West Street, where the walk turns left.

At the next bend it leaves the A1101 as it turns right, on a waymarked track. Within a few yards it turns right again, along a track to the rear of gardens and houses. Ignoring turnings off, the walk keeps ahead over a main cross-tracks, beyond which it turns right. Some 100 yards down this track, the Icknield Way Path turns off left, but the pub walk keeps ahead. Within a short distance the walk emerges to the left of the medieval church, almost opposite the pub.

Icknield Way Path – Cavenham Heath to Icklingham (1 mile)

For the route from the nature reserve on Cavenham Heath to Icklingham, see above.

From Icklingham, the last village with pubs along the Icknield Way Path, the route crosses sparsely populated forest and farmland well away from towns and villages.

Not far from Icklingham is a reconstructed Saxon village in West Stow Country Park on the fringes of King's Forest. There are good circular walks within the country park and from car parks and picnic sites within the forest.

The Icknield Way Association's Guide describes a different itinerary through King's Forest which includes West Stow Country Park. However, under the heading 'Last Leg' this book describes the existing, waymarked route through to Knettishall Heath, where the long-distance path ends.

Last Leg

Icknield Way Path – Icklingham to Knettishall Heath (17 miles)

Having turned left, behind Icklingham's medieval church, the route is joined by the Lark Valley Path as it crosses several fields before continuing along the farm road to Weatherhill Farm. After detouring round the farm buildings, it continues ahead to a T-junction, where it turns left, at the Icklingham Belts (turn right with the Lark Valley Path for West Stow Country Park). From here the route follows a track running north, through King's Forest, for over 3 miles before emerging on a road, along which it turns left.

After a short distance it turns right, on a byway signposted to Barrow Clump. Past a factory/farm, it turns right again, under power lines and along another byway. From here tracks run in more or less the same direction across arable fields to a wood, where the track stays ahead. Eventually, the route follows a track to the right of a large house, beyond which it follows a narrow drive or lane before turning right on a footpath between a cottage and a church in the isolated hamlet of Culford Heath. At a T-junction it turns left on a track leading to the busy A134, along which the route turns left. After about a mile it escapes the road as it turns right, on Euston Drove, just past the turning to RAF Honington and D House.

From here the route follows the track for about 2 miles before crossing Duke's Ride and continuing to the A1088, where it turns left, over the bridge and into Euston. Past the gates to Euston Park, where the road bends left, the route follows a track which bears left, behind the stone memorial cross and along to the backs of cottages. From here, it turns right, on a permissive track, then left, to the Euston/Rushford road, along which it turns right for over ½ mile.

Just before the road bears left, the route turns right, on a sandy track for about ½ mile. Through a gate it bends left, and continues for over a mile before running through woodland, past which it crosses the Rushford/Coney Weston road. From here it follows a path uphill, towards the top of which it follows a bank on the line of the Peddars Way Roman road. Over the rise, it crosses Knettishall Heath Country Park and, eventually, passes the Icknield Way Association's milestone which marks the end of the Icknield Way Path.

Beyond this milestone, the track continues ahead and, eventually, passes a Peddars Way information board. This National Trail follows a Romanised section of the Icknield Way to Hunstanton, on the Wash, from where it follows the Norfolk Coastal Path to Cromer.

Appendix

Icknield Way Historic Route – Information Centre, Dunstable Downs to Galley Hill, Luton (9 miles)

Over the B4541, the route turns left, on a path across a golf course. Past the clubhouse and over the fairway, it follows a track downhill to a road, along which it turns left. At a T-junction it turns left again, then right, along a track past a cemetery and allotments to a road, over which a cycle track leads to another road. Over this and past a chapel, it bears right, through a car park, then left, into a small shopping precinct. Here, the route turns left, then right, through an arch, to the main road (Watling Street). Over a pelican crossing it turns right, then left, into the gardens of Priory church.

Behind the church the route turns right, along Priory Road, then left, along St Peter's Road. At Bigthan Road it bears left, down an alley, to another road, across which it follows a track leading to the base of Blows Down. Here, the route turns left, alongside the railway and, eventually, emerges at a roundabout. From here it follows a minor road leading to a field, across which it turns left, over a railway line, then right, over the M1.

The route then turns left, down Halfway Avenue and dog-legs over the A505, down Stoneygate Road. Past the school it turns left, on a cycle path leading to a road. Past the Royal Oak, it crosses over a road and keeps ahead, past garages and along an alley to another road. Here it turns left, then right, and follows the road past Leagrave station.

At the main road it turns right, under the railway bridge. Over a pelican crossing at a roundabout, it follows Bramingham Road and turns right, along a cycle path which follows a wide, grassy corridor through this built-up area before dog-legging across another road. Over the river bridge, the route keeps ahead, up a grassy rise and straight down the middle of a recreation field, on the other side of which it crosses into Gooseberry Hill Road. From here, the route follows the road over the hill before turning right, along Grasmere Road, to the A6.

Across the main road, the route follows Weybourne Drive, from the end of which a path leads to the top of Warden Hill, where the path follows a fence past a trig point. Through a swing-gate, a path runs down to a track, along which the route turns right. Almost at the top of the hill, it turns left, on a field-edge path to another swing-gate. From here it follows a path over Galley Hill and down to another swing-gate, through which it keeps ahead, across the golf course, to a cross-tracks. Here, an Icknield Way Association information board marks the meeting of the Scenic and Historic Routes of the Icknield Way Path. (From here the route is described at the end of pub walk 6.)

The Icknield Way Path
Information and accommodation

Icknield Way Association, 19 Boundary Road, Bishops Stortford, Herts CM23 5LE (Route guide, Membership, Sweatshirts, T shirts etc) Tel: 01279 504602

Ramblers' Association, 1/5 Wandsworth Road, London SW8 2XX. Tel: 0171 5826878

Countryside Commission, Orton House, 110 Hills Road, Cambridge, Cambs CB2 1LQ. Tel: 01223 354462

East Anglia Tourist Board, Toppesfield Hall, Hadleigh, Suffolk IP7 5DN. Tel: 01473 822922

BUCKINGHAMSHIRE

Planning and Transportation Dept, County Hall, Aylesbury, Bucks HP20 1UY. Tel: 01296 383205

Accommodation en route:

Ivinghoe – Youth Hostel (YHA), The Old Brewery House. Tel: 01296 668251

BEDFORDSHIRE

Leisure Services, County Hall, Bedford, Beds MK42 9AP. Tel: 01234 363222

Tourist Information Centres for accommodation en route:

Dunstable – The Library, Vernon Place. Tel: 01582 471012
Luton – 65-67 Bute Street. Tel: 01582 401579

HERTFORDSHIRE

Countryside Management Service, County Hall, Hertford SG13 8DN. Tel: 01992 555265

Tourist Information Centres and accommodation en route:

Lilley – The Lilley Arms, West Street. Tel: 01462 768371
Ickleford – The Cricketers, 107 Arlesey Road. Tel: 01462 432629
Hitchin TIC – The Library, Paynes Park. Tel: 01462 450133
Letchworth – The Three Horseshoes Inn, Norton Road. Tel: 01462 684890
Baldock – The Rose and Crown Hotel, 8 Whitehorse Street. Tel: 01462 892339
Royston TIC – The Library, Market Hill. Tel: 01763 243292

ESSEX

Planning Dept, County Hall, Chelmsford CM1 1LF. Tel: 01245 492211

Tourist Information Centres and accommodation en route :

Elmdon – The King's Head, Heydon Lane. Tel: 01763 838358

Great Chesterford – The Crown and Thistle, High Street. Tel: 01799 530278

Saffron Walden – Youth Hostel, 1 Myddylton Place. Tel: 01799 523117

Saffron Walden TIC – Market Place. Tel: 01799 510444

CAMBRIDGESHIRE

The Rural Group, Shire Hall, Cambridge CB3 OAP. Tel: 01223 317445

Accommodation en route :

Linton – The Crown Inn, 11 High Street. Tel: 01223 891759

Balsham – Yole Farm, Linton Road. Tel: 01223 893280

Brinkley – The Red Lion. Tel: 01638 507285

Stetchworth – Live and Let Live Guest House, 76 High Street.
Tel: 01638 508153

Cheveley – The Rectory, 130 The Street. Tel: 01638 730770

SUFFOLK

County Planning, St Edmund House, County Hall, Ipswich, IP4 1LZ.
Tel: 01473 265132

Tourist Information Centres and accommodation en route:

Newmarket TIC – 63 The Rookery. Tel: 01638 667200

Moulton – Flint End House, 6 The Street. Tel: 01638 750966

Bury St Edmunds TIC – 6 Angel Hill. Tel: 01284 764667

Tuddenham – Oakdene, Higham Road. Tel: 01638 718822

Icklingham – Weatherhill Farm. Tel: 01284 728839